UK Housing

Editor: Tracy Biram

Volume 396

independence
educational publishers

First published by Independence Educational Publishers

The Studio, High Green

Great Shelford

Cambridge CB22 5EG

England

© Independence 2021

Copyright

Photocopy licence

ISBN-13: 978 1 86168 854 5

Printed in Great Britain

Zenith Print Group

Contents

Introduction

UK Housing is Volume 396 in the **issues** series. The aim of the series is to offer current, diverse information about important issues in our world, from a UK perspective.

About UK Housing

The UK has been in the midst of a housing emergency for many years. This book looks at the booming UK housing market, the shortage of affordable homes and the ever-rising need for more social housing. It also explores the pros and cons of renting vs. buying, different approaches to solving the crisis and what the future for UK housing might look like.

OUR SOURCES

Titles in the **issues** series are designed to function as educational resource books, providing a balanced overview of a specific subject.

The information in our books is comprised of facts, articles and opinions from many different sources, including:

♦ Newspaper reports and opinion pieces

♦ Website factsheets

♦ Magazine and journal articles

♦ Statistics and surveys

♦ Government reports

♦ Literature from special interest groups.

A NOTE ON CRITICAL EVALUATION

Because the information reprinted here is from a number of different sources, readers should bear in mind the origin of the text and whether the source is likely to have a particular bias when presenting information (or when conducting their research). It is hoped that, as you read about the many aspects of the issues explored in this book, you will critically evaluate the information presented.

It is important that you decide whether you are being presented with facts or opinions. Does the writer give a biased or unbiased report? If an opinion is being expressed, do you agree with the writer? Is there potential bias to the 'facts' or statistics behind an article?

ASSIGNMENTS

In the back of this book, you will find a selection of assignments designed to help you engage with the articles you have been reading and to explore your own opinions. Some tasks will take longer than others and there is a mixture of design, writing and research-based activities that you can complete alone or in a group.

FURTHER RESEARCH

At the end of each article we have listed its source and a website that you can visit if you would like to conduct your own research. Please remember to critically evaluate any sources that you consult and consider whether the information you are viewing is accurate and unbiased.

Useful Websites

www.bigissue.com

www.business.yougov.com

www.england.shelter.org.uk

www.independent.co.uk

www.insidehousing.co.uk

www.newstatesman.com

www.openaccessgovernment.org

www.pbctoday.co.uk

www.positive.news

www.shoutoutuk.org

www.telegraph.co.uk

www.theconversation.com

www.theguardian.com

www.thenegotiatior.com

www.todaysconveyancer.co.uk

www.ticfinance.co.uk

www.unbiased.co.uk

www.yougov.co.uk

How do we fix the UK housing crisis?

By Hilary Osborne, Pamela Duncan, Lydia McMullan

How do you fix a housing crisis that has its foundations in policy decisions that go back decades? Unsurprisingly, there is not one answer.

The issues of high house prices – illustrated by the large swathes of Great Britain in which key workers are priced out – as well as a lack of affordable rented homes and homelessness will need a wide range of measures to tackle. We asked experts for their ideas.

Build differently

"The UK's housing affordability crisis has been building for decades, with younger generations locked out of home ownership and spending long periods of time living in often high-cost, poor-quality private rented accommodation," says Lindsay Judge, research director at the Resolution Foundation thinktank.

"Sadly, if anything, the pandemic has made housing even less affordable for young people."

Judge says a fresh approach is needed that includes building more homes in high-demand areas of the UK, such as the major cities.

The National Housing Federation, which represents housing associations across England, suggests new skills and methods of construction could help in future. "This includes building homes in factories out of materials such as timber frames, and then assembling them on site over only a few days," the NHF says. "Such methods enable homes to be built more cheaply, to a higher standard and more quickly."

The NHF says research from the National Audit Office has suggested that if modern methods of construction are used instead of traditional bricks and mortar, it could be possible to build up to four times as many homes with the same amount of on-site labour.

Improve the private rented sector

Judge describes the private rental sector as the "'wild west' of Britain's housing stock", and the Resolution Foundation says it should be professionalised. The thinktank suggests policy should be "moving to indefinite tenancies, and creating a tenants' loans system to tackle the mounting arrears crisis without causing mass evictions".

The campaign group Generation Rent says private tenancies should be reformed. Dan Wilson Craw, the group's deputy director, says this will "give renters the certainty that they can live in their home long-term, and can plan their lives – whether or not they have a decent shot at home ownership".

Many tenancy agreements last six months, or a year, and after that households can be asked to move on. This makes it difficult for people to put down roots and for families to plan for schooling, and generally means an extra cost for renters who have to arrange a move.

"Growing numbers of renters are reaching their 40s having been unable to save enough for a deposit, with little prospect of a bank lending a mortgage if it won't be paid off until retirement age," says Wilson Craw. "They therefore face renting in insecure tenancies for the rest of their lives, and no proposed home ownership initiatives will overcome this."

There are also problems around rental deposits, with tenants asked to find a downpayment before they have money back from their existing landlords. The National Residential Landlords Association says as part of the forthcoming renters' reform bill "the government should develop either a financial bridging facility or a deposit builder Isa to make it easier for tenants to move home without needing to find money for a fresh deposit each time".

The NRLA is also calling for tenants to get more help to use existing rules that allow them to challenge rent increases they believe to be unfair in tribunals.

Overhaul property taxes and mortgages

Despite changes in recent years to rein-in buy-to-let through tax changes, Generation Rent says the system still encourages speculation in property, to the detriment of aspiring owner-occupiers.

"Landlords can get interest-only mortgages, which puts them at an advantage over owner-occupiers," says Wilson Craw. "Council tax bears little relation to a property's value, so a wealthy household can pay the same tax on a home with three spare bedrooms as a family of four crammed into a two-bedroom flat. These policies incentivise investors to put as much money into property as they can get their hands on, pushing up prices."

Help struggling renters

"The economic fallout from the pandemic has left millions of families worried about paying rent," says Darren Baxter, housing policy and partnerships manager at the Joseph Rowntree Foundation thinktank. "The government should immediately introduce a targeted package of grants to support renters in arrears, ensuring that they can stay in their homes."

In March 2020 the Local Housing Allowance (LHA) was increased to cover the bottom 30% of rents, but from April this year it will be frozen again in cash terms, meaning the gap between rental costs and support available will start to widen again. The Joseph Rowntree Foundation wants the government to reverse its decision to freeze LHA so that it is recoupled to the real cost of renting.

The NRLA says housing support in the benefits system needs to reflect the average cost of renting in any given area.

Sort out pay

High housing costs is one part of the equation, but the other is pay. In recent years wage increases have lagged behind house price rises. Many of the key workers the Guardian has included in its analysis have jobs in the public sector, where pay rises have been frozen for years.

Baxter says: "Many key workers are employed in sectors with higher levels of insecurity, low levels of pay and few opportunities to progress, such as care workers and delivery drivers.

"Alongside increasing the supply of genuinely affordable housing and better support for renters on low incomes, we need to see the social security system strengthened, employment rights improved and continued commitment to increase the national living wage."

And of course, build more affordable housing

Everyone we asked agrees that more affordable housing is needed. Currently, about half is provided by developers through section 106 agreements on new private estates and blocks. The Joseph Rowntree Foundation says plans to replace that system with a national infrastructure levy, the details of which are unclear, need to ensure that there is not even less social housing built in future.

Several of the groups which responded to us cited research for the National Housing Federation and Crisis that was carried out by Heriot-Watt University. The research says 145,000 affordable homes should be built annually for the next five years, of which 90,000 a year should be for social rent. This is the lowest-cost housing that councils and housing associations provide, with rents tied to local incomes. In recent times fewer than 7,000 new homes a year have been created in this category in England.

"The bottom line is, you cannot solve affordability without genuinely affordable homes," says the housing charity Shelter. "That means we need to address the chronic shortage of social homes in this country. This shortage is at the heart our housing emergency."

Shelter points out that building social housing will be an investment, as it will cut the housing benefits being paid to private landlords.

The Joseph Rowntree Foundation, says the rules around the right to buy should be changed, so that councils get to keep all of the money raised from sales. "The proportion that can be reinvested to build more social housing should also be increased," Baxter says.

1 April 2021

Building more homes won't solve UK housing crisis, new report argues

Despite rapid house-building, UK house prices have grown 160 per cent in real terms since their low point in 1996.

By Oleysa Dmitracova, Economics and Business Editor

Simply building more houses is not the answer to Britain's housing crisis, an economist argues, making the case instead for increasing the supply of social housing, subsidies for first-time buyers and measures to encourage private landlords to sell their properties.

UK house prices have grown 160 per cent in real terms since 1996, rents are relatively high and home ownership has fallen over the past 15 years. But, despite common perceptions, tight housing supply is not to blame, according to a 48-page report by Ian Mulheirn from the Tony Blair Institute.

"The supply shortage story is a red herring," he says.

"The real culprit for sky-high house prices is low global interest rates that have made it easy for home owners and investors to take on large amounts of mortgage debt and pay ever more for houses.

"Meanwhile, a shrinking social rented sector, cuts to housing benefit and slow wage growth among young people are making rented housing less affordable for many, even though private sector rents are stable."

The provision of new housing has outstripped the growth in the number of households in England since house prices reached their low point in 1996, with similar trends apparent in Scotland and Wales, according to the paper written for the UK Collaborative Centre for Housing Evidence. But house prices have still soared.

Mr Mulheirn accepts that building more houses would help reduce prices and rents but adds: "The available academic evidence suggests that no plausible rate of supply would significantly reverse the price growth of the past two decades."

Even building 300,000 homes a year in England – the upper end of housing need estimates – would cut house prices only by around 10 per cent over the course of 20 years, he writes.

Since current affordability problems affect mostly people on lower incomes, solving the housing crisis requires measures to help those groups, such as more social housing for rent or more generous housing benefit, the report says.

"A tighter labour market and stronger economic growth might also benefit the pay of younger people relative to others and ease affordability problems," it adds.

If the government wants to increase home ownership, it may need to do more to help first-time buyers get onto the housing ladder, according to Mr Mulheirn who was an economist at the Treasury earlier in his career.

Such help could take the form of tax relief, an equity loan guarantee as with the Help to Buy scheme, or the promotion of privately issued equity loans that have been proposed in the past, he writes.

At the same time, taxes on landlords could be raised, the paper says. Since landlords have limited pricing power to pass such costs on to tenants, this should make being a landlord less attractive and cause some of them to sell to a first-time buyer, either directly or via a chain.

The report is likely to prove controversial. For example, Help to Buy has been widely criticised for pumping up house prices. The National Audit Office also said in June that the scheme has handed billions of pounds of subsidised loans to relatively wealthy buyers, who would have been able to buy a property without help.

21 August 2019

Half of Brits say they would support a large increase in housebuilding in Britain

Brits generally support an increase of homes – just not if it results in large amounts of borrowing, smaller housing units or on top of green land.

By Lukas Paleckis, Political Research Executive

The government is set to go forward with a new planning bill, looking to modernise the planning system for housing in England. The bill, announced in the Queen's Speech, aims to increase the numbers of new homes being built by making it more difficult for local councils to block new housing schemes, ultimately quickening the application process of housing developments.

New YouGov data shows that half (53%) of Brits support a large increase in the amount of new housing being built in Britain, while 35% are opposed to the idea. When asked the same question in relation to homes being built in 'your own local area', support drops to 44%, while opposition increases to 46%. This is most likely to be due to the long observed phenomenon surrounding housebuilding called "NIMBY"ism (or "Not In My Back Yard") – the attitude many people have that building new things like houses or infrastructure is a good thing, so long as it doesn't happen anywhere near them.

The data also highlights how support for large-scale national housebuilding differs depending on circumstance.

Support for an increase in housing climbs to 55% if it means a substantial drop in house prices. Unsurprisingly, support for this particular reason is seen most highly amongst those likely to be getting started on the property ladder - 64% of those aged 18 to 24 and 58% of 25 to 49s.

Yet, support for housebuilding drastically declines if the government would need to borrow large amounts of money to fund the builds (30%) and if the housing units are smaller or there are plans for more high-rise blocks (25%).

One of the criticisms of the planning bill comes from countryside campaigners claiming property developers will now have more freedom to build over green fields and agricultural land. A mere 18% would be in support of a large increase in housebuilding if this were the case.

19 May 2021

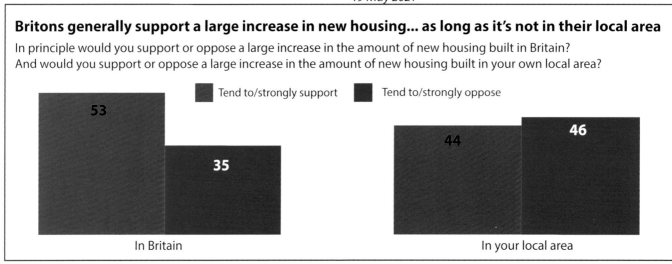

Britons generally support a large increase in new housing... as long as it's not in their local area

In principle would you support or oppose a large increase in the amount of new housing built in Britain?
And would you support or oppose a large increase in the amount of new housing built in your own local area?

Tend to/strongly support   Tend to/strongly oppose

In Britain: 53, 35
In your local area: 44, 46

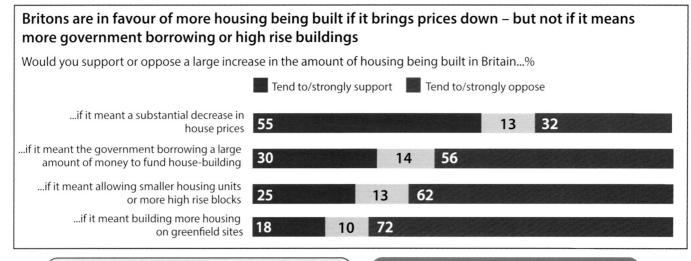

Britons are in favour of more housing being built if it brings prices down – but not if it means more government borrowing or high rise buildings

Would you support or oppose a large increase in the amount of housing being built in Britain...%

Tend to/strongly support   Tend to/strongly oppose

	Support		Oppose
...if it meant a substantial decrease in house prices	55	13	32
...if it meant the government borrowing a large amount of money to fund house-building	30	14	56
...if it meant allowing smaller housing units or more high rise blocks	25	13	62
...if it meant building more housing on greenfield sites	18	10	72

www.yougov.co.uk

17.5 million people now impacted by the housing emergency

Race, disability, sexuality and socio-economic status all barriers in the fight for a safe home

One in three adults in Britain (34%) are now impacted by the housing emergency, ground-breaking new research from Shelter shows today.

The charity questioned 13,000 people in detail about their home and housing experiences. This research has been combined with the latest government data on homelessness to expose the true extent of the housing emergency. Shockingly, when children are factored into the results, the number of people affected by Britain's housing emergency rises to 22 million.

Shelter's findings, published in its report, 'Denied the Right to a Safe Home', reveal not only the scale of the housing emergency, but also the gross inequality in the housing system:

Race: Black people are 70% more likely to be impacted by the emergency than White people; and Asian people are 50% more likely. 1m Black adults (57%) and 1.8m Asian adults (48%) do not have a safe or secure home compared with 33% of White adults.

Disability: 54% of people with a significant disability (1.8m adults) do not have a safe or secure home, compared with 30% of people without a disability.

Single mothers: 65% of single mothers (1m adults) do not have a safe or secure home, compared with 37% of two-parent households.

Socio-economic status: Low-income households on less than £20k a year are 70% more likely to be impacted than households earning £40-45k a year. (4.7m adults on a low-income do not have a safe or secure home.)

Sexuality: 40% of gay or lesbian (287,000) and 49% of bisexual people (201,000) are impacted by the emergency, compared with 32% of heterosexual people.

The research, carried out with YouGov, uses eight criteria to measure if someone has access to a safe and secure home. This includes whether their home is unaffordable, unfit or unstable, and if they have been subject to discrimination due to their race, gender, disability or sexuality.

Case study: Single mother Krystalrose, 27, privately rents a one bed flat in London with her daughter. She became homeless when pregnant and lived in a hostel before moving into her current home. There is severe mould and damp, but it is the only place Krystalrose can afford.

Krystalrose said: "I pay good money for this place - I can't afford a big food shop anymore; I really have to watch how much I eat. I thought for the amount of money it was going to be a proper home. I've tried to make it feel like one, but it's not. The mould has ruined my daughter's cot and all our clothes. We're living out of bags. I'm asthmatic and we have both become ill because of it. It's just been about coping; I'm on antidepressants now because of the stress. All I want is a home where we can feel safe and comfortable. The simple things like a wardrobe to pack your clothes away; a living room with a sofa to sit on; not having to share a bedroom. My daughter doesn't know what that feels like. It's like our lives can't move forward."

The charity's research also reveals the biggest issues people face with their housing. 11.8 million people (23%) are living in homes with significant damp, mould and condensation, or that they cannot keep warm in winter. Unaffordability and insecurity are two other key issues; four million people (8%) report regularly cutting back on essential items, like food and heating, to pay their housing costs. And four million people (8%) state they are worried about losing or being asked to leave their current home. This is largely driven by private renters who live in the least secure housing.

Shelter's report concludes Britain's housing system is unaffordable, unfit, unstable and discriminatory – a situation made even worse by the pandemic. To end the escalating housing emergency, it wants the government to build at least 90,000 good-quality social homes a year.

Polly Neate, chief executive of Shelter, said: "Decades of neglect have left Britain's housing system on its knees. A safe home is everything, yet millions don't have one. Lives are being ruined by benefit cuts, blatant discrimination and the total failure to build social homes. 23% are living in homes with significant damp, mould and condensation.

"Shelter believes a safe home is a human right, but the pain and desperation our frontline staff see every day shows this is still a long way off. That's why we are fighting for the single mum who has to put her child to bed in a room covered in mould, and the disabled man living on the twelfth floor with a broken lift. We are fighting for everyone impacted by the housing emergency - and as we emerge from the pandemic, we want the public and politicians to do the same."

With millions denied the right to a safe home, Shelter is calling on the public to join its Fight For Home and stand up against the injustice in Britain's housing system.

26 May 2021

A century of public housing: lessons from Singapore, where housing is a social, not financial, asset

THE CONVERSATION

An article from The Conversation.

By John Bryson, Professor of Enterprise and Competitiveness, University of Birmingham

One of the beacons of UK social housing policy, the legislation from 1919 that became known as the Addison Act after its sponsor, the minister of health Christopher Addison, imposed for the first time a duty on councils to build good quality and affordable housing.

But, as with most policies, it was only partially effective. Today, 100 years later, housing provision in the UK remains a major challenge, mired in problems of affordability and availability.

Britain is a home-owning nation, where housing is considered an investment asset for individuals rather than a social asset for society as a whole. This is unfortunate. As an investment, buyers pour their wealth into property on the understanding that they will benefit from rising values. The resulting price distortions lead to – among other things – localised skill shortages as key workers, teachers, nurses, firefighters are forced out by rising prices, unable to rent or buy.

But there are alternative arrangements to the hybrid housing economy that has developed in the UK – a mix of private sector ownership and renting and of housing provided by housing associations and (historically) by councils.

Housing as a social asset

Take Singapore, for example. Singapore had its own "Brexit" in 1965 when it separated from Malaysia. In 1960 the Singapore Housing and Development Board (HDB) was formed to provide affordable and high-quality housing for residents of this tiny city-state nation. Today, more than 80% of Singapore's 5.4m residents live in housing provided by the development board.

These are issued by the state on 99-year leaseholds, and the value of the home depends on the inherent utility value of the property (size, type, location), with financing readily available, including that provided by the Central Provident Fund (CPF). The CPF is a social security system that enables working Singapore citizens and those with permanent resident status to set aside funds for retirement. It is a compulsory savings scheme, which includes contributions from employers, to set aside funds for healthcare and housing costs in later life.

Property buyers in Singapore can fund the purchase of a development board flat with a bank loan, a loan from the HDB, with cash, or with funds drawn from the CPF. In a similar way to the leasehold system in the UK, the resale value of an HDB flat deteriorates as the lease end date approaches, in this case when the lease drops to under 30 years. As is the case in the UK, difficulties arise in trying to finance homes with short leases.

However, the HDB leasehold system is different as the "owners" have bought only the right to use the flat – the property title and ownership remains with HDB.

Additionally, the development board prohibits Singaporeans from owning more than two residential units at any time. In the case of an inherited flat, ownership is only allowed if the inheritor disposes of their existing private or public residential property within six months of inheriting it.

The HDB remains by far the dominant national housing provider, building and owning most residential housing and playing an extremely active role. Private sector housing is available, but it is much more expensive.

A lesson in long-termism

The differences between the approaches in the UK and Singapore are extreme. In the UK, council housing is considered to be a public sector cost – a burden to the taxpayer. For many people this is housing provision of last resort. In Singapore it is treated as an asset to the public purse, as well as a social asset – and carries no stigma, nor is seen as something to be avoided if possible. The UK's mixed housing economy results in major social and economic distortions, whereas Singapore invests in housing precisely to avoid or counter those distortions.

In the UK, with the exception of the New Towns, housing has tended to involve creating individual assets rather than an approach based on place-making – creating neighbourhoods and communities. Singapore's HDB housing units are built in HDB towns with housing units integrated with amenities including clinics, community facilities such as parks and sports facilities, and retail. As Singapore has developed economically, so HDB has also begun to produce more upmarket housing.

Transferring the solution that works for tiny Singapore to Britain would be impossible, but perhaps there are lessons to be learnt regarding a longer-term approach to meeting housing need.

One is to adopt a more integrated approach to housing: the conversation in Britain is dominated by the number of units provided and at what price they are sold, but a more sophisticated discussion would include who that housing is aimed at, where it needs to be, and how it is designed in order to create a sense of place. As important is the need to ensure housing is completely integrated into existing urban infrastructure, including roads, public transport, schools and health services.

The fragmentation of housing ownership in the UK makes it extremely expensive to redevelop or make major modifications to existing residential areas – each owner would have to be persuaded to modify their property or sell up as part of a land assembly process. In Singapore, with a history of intensifying land use and population density, HDB ownership means it is able to rebuild old estates and maintain and develop the extent of integration with social amenities.

Major innovations are occurring that will transform the ways in which we live – and these must be reflected in our housing: more electric vehicles and driverless cars, home working, e-commerce and ever-increasing population densities in cities. The integrated approach of HDB means Singapore is able to take a long-term strategic approach to these changes – and so more easily ensure that residential areas have all the public amenities, public services, retail and transport infrastructure required for them to thrive. The UK would be wise to watch and learn.

31 July 2019

Home Truths by Liam Halligan: how money rules the UK's housing shortage

The United Kingdom has faced a chronic housing shortage since the global financial crash of 2008. Since then, the economics relating to properties has spiralled out of control. Liam Halligan's *Home Truths: The UK's Chronic Housing Shortage – how it Happened, why it Matters and the Way to Solve it* takes an in-depth economic and political look at the much-discussed housing scarcity and what can be done about it.

By Sadie Trent, BA Politics and International Relations student at University of The West of England, Bristol

Shocking home truths

It is shocking to see how much house prices can vary for different parts of the country. It is a fact that the price of renting, buying, or both in some cases, has increased faster than wages and income. According to Full Fact, the average real wage fell from the start of the global financial crash of 2008 until mid-2014. However, as Halligan notes, the average UK home costs eight times someone's annual earnings. In this case, the cost of living is not being matched with people's wages. In Bridgwater, where I was born and still live today, the average rent price for a two-bedroom house is around £725 per month. In most parts of London, the same type of property will cost you in excess of £1500 per month. Bridgwater is a town in rural Somerset on a commuter route between Taunton and London, whilst London is the capital city. That is their primary difference between the two locations when it comes to pricing.

One of the defining housing policies of the Thatcher era was the Housing Act of 1980. This gave five million people in England and Wales the right to buy their council homes. A Conservative government held power in the early-to-late '90s with Norman Lamont and Sir Ken Clarke as Chancellors, until New Labour took over in 1997.

Halligan provides some interesting statistics to mull over for this period. For instance, during the early 1990s (the decade I was born in), up to 36 per cent of people aged between 16-24 owned their own home. House prices in the '90s were low enough, so young people found it easier to get onto the housing ladder faster and cheaper. One of Halligan's more interesting observations is that homeownership among this age group has plunged tenfold, resulting in housing insecurity.

NIMBY: home truths and local issues

There is much talk about NIMBYISM (Not In My Back Yard-ism) in the book. A prime example of this is the Notaro group, which is based in Bridgwater but also has offices in Weston-Super-Mare. The fallout with Notaro began in 2014 when most Somerset villages saw some of the worst floodings they had ever seen. This was the moment when it became evident that the Notaro family only cared about themselves. No one knew the lengths the Notaros would go to in order to protect their house. So, when they built a dam around its perimeter to safeguard the property from rising floodwaters, residents didn't object until it was too late. The Notaros saved themselves whilst leaving the villagers of Moorland behind. Fast-forward to 2017, despite being in property development, the Notaro group was named the ninth fastest growing business in 'healthcare', because they have a number of care homes attached to hospitals in Somerset.

An entire chapter of Halligan's book is dedicated to the fact that when people say there is no housing shortage, that is entirely false. In Bridgwater alone, there are at least four different housing estate building projects on the go with Persimmon and Taylor Wimpey. On average, people in Sedgemoor district are having to wait up to four years for a house in their banded system owing to the chronic shortage of social housing in this conservative stronghold. Interestingly, the council and EDF Energy were pleading for spare rooms for Hinkley Point C workers and were willing to offer up to £700 a month — above-average rent for Somerset. The request was successful, which begs the question: why were EDF workers fast-tracked and given housing while others on the housing list had to wait years? The same land that was used to build accommodation for the workers could have been used to build flats for the people on waiting lists.

The book for you?

Readers that want to get an economic perspective on the housing crisis will find what they're looking for in *Home Truths* with its carefully researched facts and eye-opening statistics. Looking at Britain's housing crisis from an economic perspective is immensely useful. What we get is a numbers-driven exploration of how monetary factors often impede and exacerbate this ongoing problem.

27 July 2021

Bubble trouble brewing in the housing market

With property prices around the world now growing by double digits, how big a risk are central banks running?

By Russell Lynch, Economics Editor

Nearly 15 years after a burst housing bubble tipped the world into the worst financial crisis for a century, booming property markets are triggering an uncomfortable sense of déjà vu.

From New Zealand to South Korea, prices are soaring. An Auckland fixer-upper, which couldn't even boast its own toilet, changed hands for more than NZ$2m (£1.1m) this month; meanwhile 6,000 miles away in Seoul, authorities are racing to curb an overheating market. In the US, prices are rising at the fastest pace for more than 30 years, and over here a buyer "frenzy" has driven the busiest first half on record, according to property website Rightmove.

Agent Knight Frank sees further signs of the froth in its latest global cities index, which monitors prices in 150 major markets and is now rising at its fastest pace since 2006. Kate Everett-Allen, head of international research, says: "There are now 43 cities in the index which are seeing double-digit price growth. Before the pandemic, there was just one."

The price surges come as builders scramble for materials and labour to meet the demand.

It also comes against the backdrop of stimulus poured on by policy makers warily watching the spread of the delta variant.

Former Bank of England rate setter Adam Posen warns that housing bubbles "almost always mean trouble" and puts the risk of one in the US at "seven out of 10". Are central bankers in danger of taking their eye off the ball and fuelling another crisis in the housing market?

The Bank of England insists not, despite lender Nationwide's house price index growing at its fastest pace in almost 17 years in June. Its latest Financial Stability Report barely mentions the residential housing market. Sir Jon Cunliffe, deputy governor for financial stability, is "by no means complacent" but says rate setters would "see how the market plays out" as temporary factors like the UK's stamp duty holiday are withdrawn.

He adds structural shifts could keep prices high as working from home becomes a bigger part of the economy. The big worry for the Bank – that a more buoyant market translates into higher household indebtedness – "hasn't happened so far".

But while the US Federal Reserve buys up $40bn (£29bn) a month in mortgage-backed securities as part of its Covid stimulus, other central banks are already leaning against their housing markets. The Reserve Bank of New Zealand, where prices were already inflated by a chronic shortage of supply and rock bottom borrowing costs, has reimposed loan to value limits on mortgages, ended quantitative easing (QE) and signalled that rates could rise as soon as next month.

House price stability has now been added to its mandate amid concerns over the potential damage to the financial system. In Canada, another hotspot where booming prices and a dearth of homes have prompted billboard protests from those shut out of the market, the central bank began reining in support back in April.

Adam Slater, lead economist at Oxford Economics, warns that house prices in advanced economies could be around 10pc overvalued, based on a study of markets in 14 countries.

That is yet to reach the estimated overvaluation of some 13-15pc in the run-up to the financial crisis in 2006 – but the question remains over what happens next.

He says: "The key point about this is that we're in the middle of quite a strong rise in house prices, but we don't know where the end point is. But the boom might go on for another two years, in which case these measures would look a little bit more worrying."

Slater adds: "There is a fairly widespread opinion that much of the heat in the housing market is to do with tax incentives and it will fall away once those come to an end. I think the problem with that is that if we look at a global comparison, we see the price going up rapidly in a lot of places where those tax incentives are not in place.

"Part of the reason asset prices are strong is because monetary policy is loose. It's not just housing prices that are going up, equity prices are strong as well. You can look across a variety of asset prices and find a pretty strong picture. Housing is part of that."

Experts say that the saving grace – so far at least – is a lack of leverage in the property market compared to the run-up to 2008. Mortgage credit as a share of GDP remains below levels reached before the GFC and is only exaggerated more recently by the catastrophic collapse in growth caused by coronavirus lockdowns.

Lending growth is slower than the pre-crisis period and compared with 2007-8, when a structured finance boom caused plummeting underwriting standards and surging "subprime" debt. Better-capitalised lenders have also been much more cautious about who they lend to.

In the US almost three-quarters of mortgage lending by value is going to those with an Experian "very good" credit

score, with subprime virtually non-existent. Bank of America data also shows just 2pc of new US loans are floating rate compared to above 20pc before 2007, vastly reducing the exposure of borrowers to an interest rate shock.

Bank of England figures moreover show that the share of all mortgage deals with a loan to value ratio of more than 90pc dropped in the first quarter to just 1.1pc, the lowest since it began collecting data in 2007.

"Relative to history, high LTV lending is tiny, so even in the event of a sharp house price correction, bank losses will be small," says Investec's banking analyst, Ian Gordon. But he argues that the Government is unlikely to achieve its ambitions of building 300,000 homes a year by the middle of the decade. Unemployment is set to be far lower than feared at the start of the pandemic, meaning fewer distressed sellers. "In a 'low' interest rate environment, which I see as permanent, the ability to service higher mortgage debt arguably offers some measure of housing market support," he adds.

Another factor working against the imminent pop of a bubble is the absence of a building frenzy. Everett-Allen says: "We've not had that big boom in supply that we did in a number of markets that we did before 2008. Spain and Ireland, for example, were seeing huge numbers of new build properties come to the market."

David Miles, a housing market economist and another former Bank rate-setter, says the recent price surge also has to be put in the wider context of falling real interest rates since the mid-1980s, as the yields or returns on inflation-proof government debt sank almost six percentage points. That shift inflates the prices of assets like housing, which have doubled in real terms since 1985. "The bigger picture of why house prices have gone up so much in so many countries over quite a long period now has as a relatively straightforward answer, which is that real interest rates are super low."

But Miles adds that the UK housing market is "more susceptible" to a change in the trajectory of interest rates, while his former MPC colleague Posen – now president of the Washington-based Peterson Institute for International Economics – adds that it is too early to write off bubble fears.

He says: "As we saw in the UK over the last 15 years, supply factors are not automatically self-correcting for residential investment, and can feed bubbles."

That said, the bigger threat might be from commercial property than house prices, according to TS Lombard economist Dario Perkins, as working from home trends mean more empty space and falling valuations. That puts a hole in bank balance sheets and forces companies borrowing against buildings to put up more collateral.

"There is a secular change in residential property markets, and there is also a secular change in commercial property and we don't really know how that's going to play out. If everyone is downsizing trying to get costs down, then you're talking about rising vacancy rates."

So far a combination of cheap mortgages, loose monetary policy and a lack of supply should reduce the risk of a "violent correction", according to Slater.

But US Treasury Secretary Janet Yellen has voiced concerns about the longer-term housing affordability, while Miles has warned that the benefits of buoyant house prices will be passed down to future generations "unevenly". Even if the bubble doesn't burst in dramatic 2007 fashion, the Covid property boom threatens to entrench inequalities brought to the fore by the pandemic.

24 July 2021

Will anything ever stop the madness of the British housing market?

In the last year, the average house has earned more than the average worker – and the government is to blame.

By Jonn Elledge

Sometimes, things become memes for a reason. In the financial year ending March 2020 – that is, the year before the pandemic – the median household income in the UK was £29,900. In the year to June 2021 – after the pandemic – the average price of the house that contained the average household increased by £31,000. That took it to a record high of £266,000.

In other words, at a time when incomes are under pressure from a virus that has made the entire economy sick, the average house has earned more than the average household. This little factoid pops up so often that it should be getting dull. Somehow, though, it never ceases to be shocking.

(Yes, I am conflating median with mean there. I will apologise for this just as soon as the multimillionaire Chancellor of the Exchequer Rishi Sunak apologises for thinking higher housing costs are a good thing.)

Remarkably, that isn't even the worst thing about the latest house price figures dropped by the Office for National Statistics this week. The worst thing is best summed up by this headline from the Guardian's economics editor Larry Elliott: "UK house prices rise at fastest rate since 2004". Can you think of anything that might have happened in the economy or the housing market after 2004 that might make this phenomenon a tiny bit worrying?

There are people in the property industry who certainly think so. George Franks, a cofounder of the London-based estate agent Radstock Properties – the sort of company that tends to be in favour of ever-higher house prices – described the increase as "frankly obscene". Others are more sanguine, by which I mean very obviously delighted. Nicky Stevenson, the managing director of another estate agent, Fine & Country, noted that,

"While we expect things to steady later in the year, there is nothing in this data to suggest the brakes will be applied heavily to what has become a runaway market." Let joy be unconfined.

Reading between the lines of Stevenson's comment, you get the impression she's a little disappointed that London has seen a relatively modest price increase of just 6.3 per cent, compared with 13.2 per cent in the UK as a whole, making it the least boom-y region of the country this year. You don't have to look hard for a reason: the pandemic-driven trend towards home-working, combined with the lengthy shutdowns of social and cultural venues, has left many Londoners wondering whether it's really worth paying quite so much for a shoebox with no garden, and whether it might be time to move out.

This is perhaps the reason why, in the two regions around London – the south-east and east of England – house prices climbed by 10.5 and 12.1 per cent respectively in the year to June 2021. That's nothing compared with much of England, though: house prices climbed by 14.3 per cent in the East

House price growth has significantly outpaced wage growth

UK average house prices and weekly earnings, indexed to Jan 1970

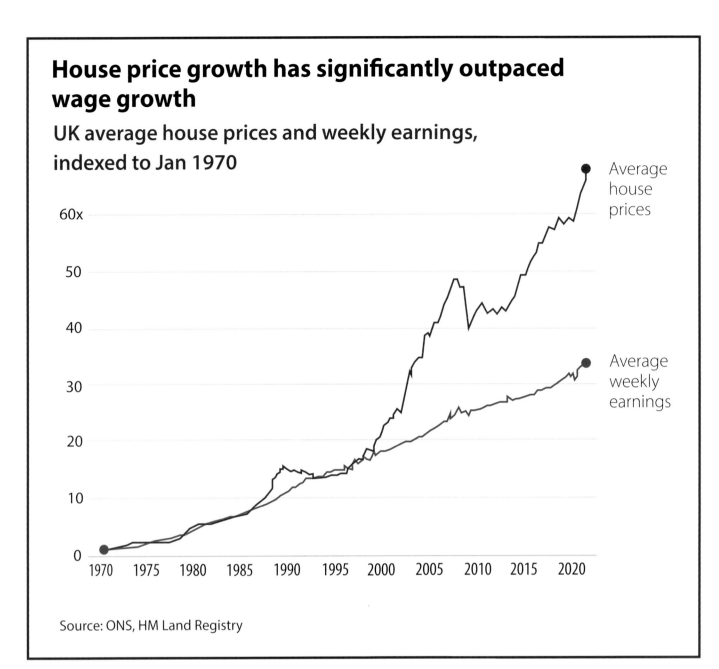

Source: ONS, HM Land Registry

Midlands, 15 per cent in the West Midlands, 15.8 per cent in Yorkshire, and a frankly absurd 18.6 per cent in the north-west. Even without a pandemic to contend with, it seems highly unlikely that pay packets would have risen at the same rate. But we do have a pandemic to contend with, which makes things worse.

Don't worry too much about the poor, left-behind homeowners of the capital, though: the average London house price in June stood at a record high of £510,299, so it's in no immediate danger of losing its crown as the country's most unaffordable region. As the Economist's Duncan Weldon noted: the increase in the value of the average London property since 2006 would, by itself, be enough to buy you two average homes in the north-east.

And remember: this boom in house prices, unaccompanied by a boom in incomes, has once again been engineered entirely deliberately, as a way of kick-starting a sluggish economy and to hell with the consequences. Where George Osborne did it using Help to Buy, Sunak used temporary cuts to stamp duty to give the impression that bargains were on offer. Given those cuts' impact on house prices, it's very far from clear that this was so.

The stamp duty holiday is winding down now. Perhaps that will mean a sudden dip in house prices, leading to instability, negative equity and, quite possibly, recession. Then again, perhaps it won't – in which case the Chancellor has successfully made housing even more expensive, and put homeownership out of reach for yet more young renters. (It's striking that, when Stevenson predicts London prices might rise faster in the autumn, she expects investors from the Gulf to prop up the market.)

Both these options seem plausible. Neither are good. And either way, it's Rishi Sunak who should get the blame.

20 August 2021

The ultimate list of UK housing statistics 2021

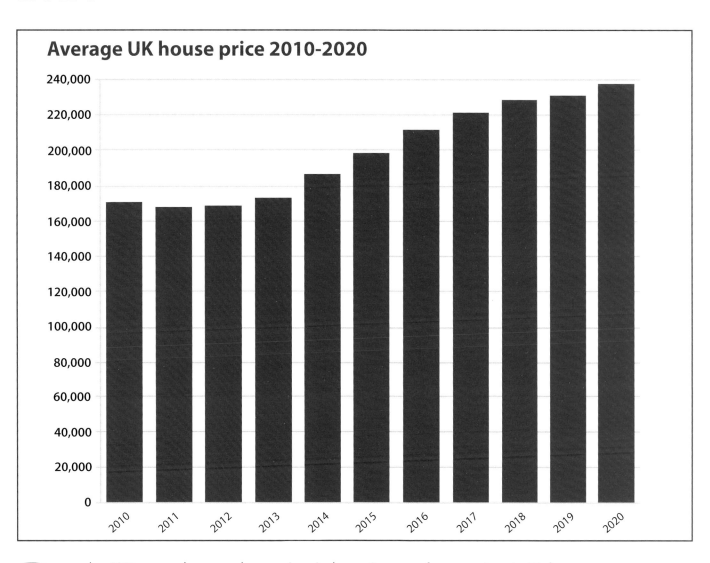

Average UK house price 2010-2020

December 2020 saw yearly average house prices rise by 8.5%, the highest percentage increase since October 2014. This has mostly been due to the Stamp Duty Land Tax (SDLT) holiday which has encouraged sellers to increase asking prices thanks to reduced purchasing costs.

The average UK house price is now around £252,000, an almost £100,000 increase in the last 10 years.

Average house prices in England

♦ House prices in England grew by 8.5% in the year to December 2020. The current average value stands at £269,000.

♦ This represents an average increase of £21,000 per home.

Average house prices in London

♦ In November 2020, the average house price in London rose over £500,000 for the first time in history, however, London prices closed out the year at £496,000.

♦ London prices grew by 3.5% in the year to December 2020, which was the lowest growth rate of any region in the UK.

Average house prices in Wales

♦ Houses in Wales saw the steepest increase in price, growing by 10.7% in the year to December 2020.

♦ The average house in Wales currently costs £184,000, a record high for the region.

Average house prices in Scotland

♦ Scotland's house prices grew by 8.4%, close to the national average.

♦ The average property in Scotland costs £163,000 as of December 2020, this is slightly down from the peak of £164,000 in November 2020.

Average house prices in Northern Ireland

♦ Northern Ireland is still the cheapest country in the UK to purchase a house in, with the average house price ending 2020 at £148,000.

♦ This represents a 5.3% increase over the year to quarter 4, as Northern Ireland's house price data is collected quarterly, unlike the other countries of the union.

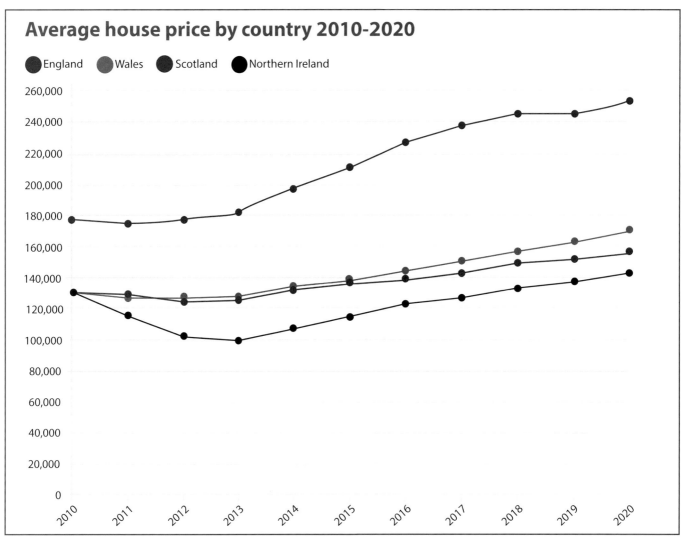

Average house price by country 2010-2020

● England ● Wales ● Scotland ● Northern Ireland

Covid impact on sales

The measures introduced last March to curb the spread of coronavirus had a significant impact on house sales as most sales were prohibited during the initial lockdown. However, the pent-up demand following this period, as well as the Stamp Duty holiday and savings from reduced commutes and closed bars and restaurants, actually resulted in more mortgage approvals than 2019.

The Stamp Duty holiday means any property below the value of £500,000 is no longer required to pay the additional tax when purchased. Previously the SDLT threshold was £125,000. The scheme is expected to end in April 2021, meaning any property purchase not completed by March 31st will again be subject to the lower threshold.

Average house price per region

House prices grew the most in the North West, where the average property is 11.2% more expensive than it was in December 2019. London saw the lowest growth at 3.5% but London remains the most expensive place to buy property in the UK.

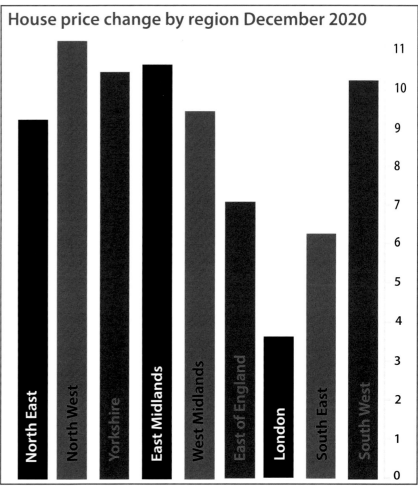

House price change by region December 2020

Cheapest counties

Rank	Local authority	Average house price	Y-O-Y change
1	Blaenau Gwent	£90,000	+1
2	Burnley	£95,000	-1
3	Hyndburn	£110,000	-
4	Pendle	£112,500	+4
5	Merthyr Tydfil	£115,000	+2
5	Rhondda Cynon Taff	£115,000	New
6	Blackpool	£118,000	+4
7	County Durham	£119,000	-3
8	Stoke-on-Trent	£120,000	New
8	Kingston upon Hull	£120,000	New
8	Blackburn with Darwen	£120,000	New

Blaenau Gwent takes over from Burnley as the cheapest area of England and Wales to buy a house in 2020.

New entrants to the cheapest areas include Rhondda, Stoke on Trent, Hull and Blackburn

Most expensive counties

Rank	Local authority	Average house price	Y-O-Y change
1	Kensington and Chelsea	£1,275,000	-
2	Westminster	£989,995	-
3	City of London	£815,000	-
4	Camden	£788,000	-
5	Hammersmith and Fulham	£740,000	-
6	Wandsworth	£743,500	+4
7	Hackney	£640,460	New
8	Richmond upon Thames	£640,000	-2
9	Islington	£620,000	-2
10	Elmbridge	£574,342	-2

Mostly unchanged in the most expensive areas of England and Wales, with only one new entrant, Hackney, which has seen an increase of almost £100,000 in the year ending June 2020

Elmbridge in Surrey is the only area outside of London to make the top 10.

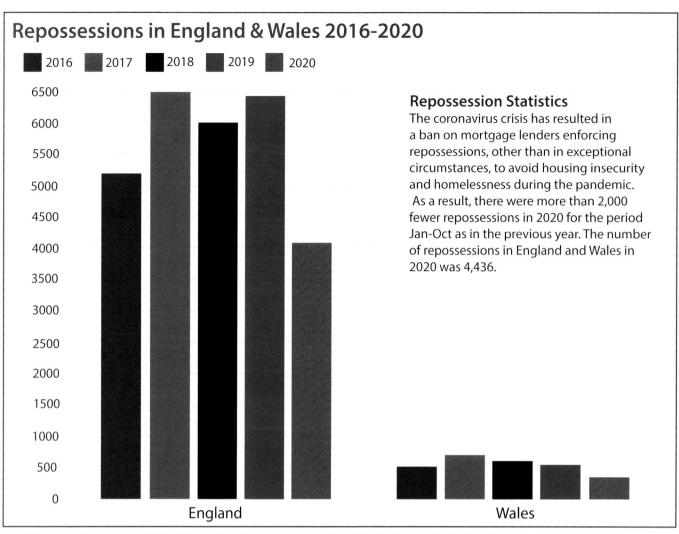

Repossessions in England & Wales 2016-2020

Legend: 2016, 2017, 2018, 2019, 2020

Repossession Statistics

The coronavirus crisis has resulted in a ban on mortgage lenders enforcing repossessions, other than in exceptional circumstances, to avoid housing insecurity and homelessness during the pandemic. As a result, there were more than 2,000 fewer repossessions in 2020 for the period Jan-Oct as in the previous year. The number of repossessions in England and Wales in 2020 was 4,436.

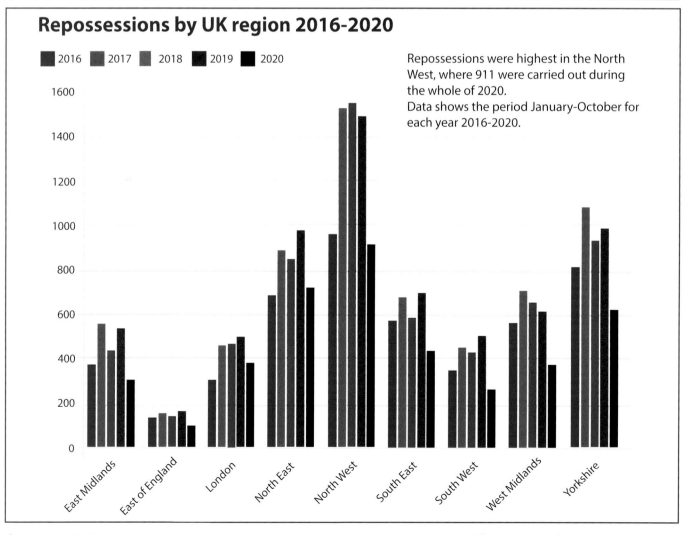

Repossessions by UK region 2016-2020

Legend: 2016, 2017, 2018, 2019, 2020

Repossessions were highest in the North West, where 911 were carried out during the whole of 2020.

Data shows the period January-October for each year 2016-2020.

Mortgage statistics

The number of mortgage approvals in 2020 was 818,500, a 3.7% increase. This is the largest number of approvals in a single year since 2007.

Net mortgage borrowing in 2020 totalled £43.3 billion, a significant drop from 2019, where net borrowing totalled £48.1 billion.

Approvals for remortgaging stood at 451,400 in the year to December 2020, down by 23% compared with the 587,600 approved in 2019.

First-time buyers

The English Housing Survey 2019-2020 found that there were 827,000 first time buyers in England, 100,000 more than the previous year.

The average age of a first-time buyer in the UK has fallen from 33 in 2018-2019 to 32 in 2019-2020.

The average deposit for first-time buyers was £42,433, a 12.6% drop from the previous period.

The number of first time buyers relying on savings to pay their deposit has grown slightly in the past year, while the number using a gift or loan from friends or family has dropped in 2020.

2021

Sources

https://www.bankofengland.co.uk/statistics/money-and-credit/2020/december-2020

https://www.ons.gov.uk/

https://www.gov.uk/government/collections/english-housing-survey

Renting vs buying: should I get a mortgage?

With property prices around the world now growing by double digits, how big a risk are central banks running?

By Nick Green, Financial Journalist

According to the HomeOwners Alliance, 86% of people in Britain want to own their own home. But with house prices continuing to rise, becoming a first-time buyer is prohibitively expensive for many. There's also the responsibility of taking on a long-term loan. Are there any instances when renting is actually the better option? Let's take a look.

What are the advantages of buying a house?

There are clearly many more factors other than cost that will determine the best option for you. Here are the main upsides of home ownership.

♦ **Security:** You can't be made to move out at short notice by a landlord.

♦ **Freedom:** You don't have to stick to a tenancy agreement that sets out what you can and cannot do, and you can decorate and furnish your home exactly to your taste and make structural modifications to enhance its value.

♦ **It's an investment in your future:** Instead of paying rent that pays off your landlord's mortgage, your monthly payments will be contributing towards something that is yours. In the long-term, you could use the equity from your home to buy a bigger house as your circumstances change or downsize to fund your retirement. For many people, the most money they make in their lives is from the rising value of their home.

♦ **Control:** With a fixed-rate mortgage, you can control your costs more easily than being at the whim of a landlord who may suddenly put your rent up.

What are the disadvantages of buying a house?

For all that home ownership is an ambition for so many of us, there are significant drawbacks to it as well:

♦ **It's a big financial commitment:** As well as having to save for a deposit (a 10% down payment on a £250,000 home is a whopping £25,000), you'll have to be sure you can meet the monthly mortgage payments. If you stretch your budget when you buy, you might not have money for treats such as meals out and holidays. And, if your financial circumstances change – for example, if you lose your job or interest rates rise – and you struggle to pay your mortgage, your home could be repossessed, which can also affect your access to credit in the future.

♦ **The property market can change:** While the overall trend for property is that it rises in value over the long-term, it's a volatile market. If prices take a tumble, you might end up with 'negative equity', where your home is worth less than your mortgage, making it very difficult to sell.

♦ **Additional costs:** You'll need extra insurance to cover buildings as well as contents and term life insurance to protect your mortgage if something happens to you. The costs of maintaining your home – such as fixing the roof or repairing the boiler – will all have to be met by you as the homeowner.

♦ **Less flexibility:** Selling up and moving is more expensive when you own a home than when you're renting as you have estate agency and legal fees to pay. If you're living with someone and split up, deciding what to do with the property can be complicated and costly.

What are the advantages of renting?

Now let's see the areas where renting a home may be a better fit for some people's lifestyles.

- ◆ **Flexibility:** Most rental contracts are 12-months long, which means that If you change jobs or just want to try living in a different area, it's easier to move quickly. If you lose your job, you can give your landlord notice, walk away and rent something smaller or move in with family or friends temporarily.

- ◆ **Maintenance is not your responsibility:** When you live in rented accommodation, and there's something wrong such as a broken shower or a mysterious leak under the sink, you just have to contact the landlord to sort it out.

- ◆ **Budgeting is easier:** You know what your rent will be each month and, if your landlord manages your utilities for you too, you know what your electric, water and other household bills will be and how much disposable income you have to spend on doing the things you enjoy.

- ◆ **Location, location, location:** Some of the UK's most desirable locations are out of reach for most home buyers, whereas renting enables you to live in more sought-after areas. For example, if you fancy London's trendy Bethnal Green, the average price for a two-bedroom house is an eye-watering £649,077. For comparison, renting a two-bed property there costs around £1,848 a month. And though this may work out as more than your mortgage repayments might be, you wouldn't need to find the huge deposit that you'd also need to buy a property there.

What are the disadvantages of renting?

It's no secret that there are plenty of downsides to renting, but let's run through them anyway in order to make a clear comparison.

- ◆ **You're paying your landlord's mortgage rather than your own:** Every month's rent payment goes to your landlord rather than being used to help you become a homeowner yourself and building up a potential nest egg for your future.

- ◆ **You have to abide by the tenancy rules:** There are likely to be restrictions on things such as owning pets or modifying the property.

- ◆ **Your rent can go up on the whim of your landlord:** Your monthly rent can be subject to sudden increases, which could unexpectedly impact your monthly budgeting.

- ◆ **Insecurity:** When your tenancy comes to an end, your landlord may not carry you over on to the next lease or may suddenly decide to sell the property. Either way, you may have to quickly find somewhere else to live.

What's cheaper – buying or renting?

In the short term, renting can be cheaper as, in addition to your deposit, fees and surveys, there are some extra costs you'll have as a homeowner, such as buildings and life insurance, and property maintenance, which you don't have when renting.

However, when interest rates are low, and if you have a big deposit, homeownership can prove cheaper than renting in terms of monthly repayments. You'll also have the added

benefit of owning an asset that should steadily rise in value over time.

According to the Office for National Statistics (ONS), the average UK house price in January 2021 was £249,000. Along with a 10% deposit of £24,900, consumer organisation Which? calculates the costs of mortgage fees and charges, valuation fees, survey costs, conveyancing fees and removals costs, as coming in between £1,330 and £6,140. At the top end, this means you'll need funds of more than £30,000 to be able to buy your own home. Then, you'll have to find £1,062.71 a month, based on a 25-year interest-only mortgage. If interest rates rise by 3%, this will increase to £1,443.88 a month.

The ONS calculates that the average monthly rent in England, recorded between 1 April 2019 and 31 March 2020, was £700, although this varies significantly from region to region. Unsurprisingly, London had the highest average monthly rent at £1,425, while the North East had the lowest average monthly rent at £495. When renting, you'll normally be required to pay one to two months' rent in advance, along with a tenancy deposit, which must be no more than five weeks' rent.

In summary: buying requires a bigger upfront cost, but renting is more expensive in the long term. A good rule of thumb is that buying a property becomes better value after around 10 years, compared to renting an identical property.

Whether it's cheaper to buy or rent depends on several factors. If you decide you'd like to buy, the best way to find the right mortgage deal for you is to use an independent mortgage broker who has access to the whole of the mortgage market and can maximise your chances of a successful application.

Nick Green is a financial journalist writing for Unbiased.co.uk, the site that has helped over 10 million people find financial, business and legal advice. Nick has been writing professionally on money and business topics for over 15 years, and has previously written for leading accountancy firms PKF and BDO.

22 April 2021

Global: who does – and doesn't – want to own a home?

YouGov Profiles data shows that, among people who don't currently own a home, three quarters (76%) want to.

By Christien Pheby

Home ownership is often seen as the holy grail of domesticity: it's an asset, a milestone, and a route out of filling up some faceless landlord's bank account at the expense of your own. But it also comes with its own costs and burdens: when the water heater is broken, the kitchen needs refitting, and no toilet in the house will flush properly, the benefits of having a place to call your own can seem remote indeed.

Across all 17 markets featured in our study, just over half (53%) own their own house. Home ownership is highest in Singapore (65%) and Sweden (63%), and lowest in Germany (34%) and the UAE (32%), but in most of these countries, regions or areas, it's more common to own your home than not.

When it comes to people who don't own their own home, most want to: three-quarters (76%) say they want to have their own property in future, while 15% do not. The dream of home ownership is especially potent in Indonesia (95%) and Mexico (94%); in both markets, just 2% do not aspire to have their own house someday. In other markets, it's a more mixed story. People who don't have property generally aspire to it – but the degree varies heavily, especially within Europe. While 84% of Spaniards want to own their own home, this falls to just two-thirds of Danes (66%), three in five French people (62%), and less than half of Germans (48%).

Germans are, by some distance, the group most likely to eschew home ownership: two in five (42%) say they have no intention of buying property. This may be due to the country's anomalous housing policies, including higher real estate taxes, wide access to social housing, and a lack of mortgage interest deductions for owner-occupiers.

So while Germany is an outlier, it is also an example of a country where housing policy has given people more reason to rent and less reason to want a house of their own. While there are sentimental reasons to buy a house, it's also a practical decision influenced by the benefits accorded to homeowners by society. When those benefits don't exist, interest in owning a house may drop significantly.

29 June 2021

Global: home ownership

Singapore	65
Sweden	63
Great Britain	62
Denmark	61
France	58
Hong Kong	57
Italy	57
USA	56
Australia	55
Spain	55
China	53
India	49
Poland	48
Mexico	44
Indonesia	35
Germany	34
UAE	32
All	53

Why more people want to live in tiny houses

People I have spoken to who build tiny homes cite a desire for simplicity and a move away from a life focused on spending and buying, writes Alice Elizabeth Watson.

By Alice ELizabeth Watson

Tiny houses have been heralded as a radical and creative way to address a lack of affordable housing, as well as reducing living costs and shrinking our carbon footprint.

My PhD research looks at the tiny house movement in the UK. I am interested in who lives in them and why, and in the barriers that people face to living in this way.

I am also building my own tiny house at the same time. I am excited by the idea that people could build their own houses – it is a lot of fun – and halve their living costs at the end.

Yet my research is also highlighting that for many people, living in a tiny home is an act of necessity. It's not that they want to live in a 5m x 5m timber box, it's that they can't afford to do anything else. And for others, even this is out of reach.

Tiny houses are homes usually 40sq m or less. A popular construction style is to build them on a trailer base. This allows them to be classified as road-towable vehicles, and avoids many of the complications of building a permanent home with foundations. Others are log-cabin style or shed homes, and some are even built underground.

They are much cheaper than traditional housing – the average tiny house price tends to be around £35,000 – and result in much cheaper living costs. This can free up time from the obligation to work to pay rent or a mortgage.

Research has suggested that people who live in tiny houses spend more time outside or with friends and family, which can make them happier than their overworked counterparts.

However, building a tiny house still requires thousands of pounds and, importantly, somewhere to build. This means these projects seem mostly to be done by people who do have some savings, access to personal loans, and friends or family who own land. It's just that they don't have enough savings to buy a "real" house.

This means that although tiny houses are considerably more affordable than conventional houses, they are out of the reach of the people who are in most dire need of housing.

If somebody is unable to save up the average deposit for a brick house, they are not likely to be able to summon this amount for a tiny house either. What's more, you can't borrow money through conventional mortgages to build tiny houses because they are not attached to land, which is the real asset that appreciates in value over time.

My participants have described tiny houses as a way to reduce living costs in such a way that they can either work much less, or work in more fulfilling jobs for a lower salary

Instead, tiny houses must be financed via private loans, just like if you wanted to buy a car. A typical interest rate on a mortgage loan in the UK right now is roughly 2 per cent.

Compare this to the interest you would have to pay on a personal loan to build your tiny house – an average of 7 per cent – and it becomes clear how unfavourable the financial landscape is for this type of project.

Of course, tiny homes can be built for significantly less than the average price. A participant in my research study built a 10sq m tiny house for just £900. He loves this home and spends a lot of time in it. However, it is built on land that he already owns – another hurdle to overcome which is eased by material capital.

The UK has the longest average working hours in Europe, and a significant proportion of earnings go towards housing costs.

"My participants have described tiny houses as a way to reduce living costs in such a way that they can either work much less, or work in more fulfilling jobs for a lower salary."

People have expressed to me how they found it strange that they used to work 40 hours per week to pay for a home they were seldom in.

Recommended

People I have spoken to who build tiny homes cite a desire for simplicity and a move away from a life focused on spending and buying. Some have described the work-to-spend attitude of society as unfulfilling and harmful.

It seems counterintuitive that people would prefer less space to more, and that people would volunteer to live in a shed on wheels if there were enough affordable homes. Yet I have encountered people who do have the money to live in a conventionally sized house but would prefer to live tiny – and find their goals obstructed by planning permission and access to land.

Another way to look at the tiny house movement is that it sums up the failures of adequate distribution of resources and access to opportunity. It can be seen to be romanticising poverty and ignoring structural inequality. The movement is known to be fairly white and middle-class, which suggests its radical potential is being overstated.

Alice Elizabeth Wilson is a PhD Researcher in Sociology at the University of York. This article first appeared on The Conversation.

15 May 2020

The micro homes designed to tackle the UK housing crisis

Nine of the eco-friendly dwellings are being mooted for brownfield land in Bristol. Could the concept help other UK cities create much-needed affordable housing?

By Gavin Haines

Being smart with space is a necessity in densely populated cities, yet awkward slivers of brownfield land remain a common sight in many urban areas.

Often overlooked for being too small or difficult to build on, such plots can remain in a state of neglect for years. Meanwhile, people struggle to get on the housing ladder due to a lack of affordable homes.

Offering a potential solution to these twin problems is a new micro housing project called 'gap homes', featuring properties that can be dropped into tight urban spaces.

A consultation is currently under way to install nine of the dwellings on brownfield land in Bristol. The proposed site was previously occupied by dilapidated council garages, which were recently pulled down.

Plans for the development feature communal gardens and outdoor seating areas to encourage residents to mingle. The two-storey homes also feature PV solar panels and airsource heat pumps to reduce their environmental impact.

The homes would be owned by Bristol city council and assembled in a factory.

"Manufacture of the houses would largely be carried out off-site, which would cause less disruption than a traditional build during the construction phase," said the council in its consultation.

The gap homes concept was designed by BDP architects to help ease the housing crisis in Bristol, which like most UK cities, has a lack of affordable properties.

"It will bring new energy and life, revitalising neighbourhoods."

BDP said the homes would help revitalise neighbourhoods in Bristol and potentially beyond. With an estimated 2,000 council garages located across the city, there is certainly potential for the concept to be scaled-up locally.

"Placing these new, attractive and carefully designed houses in their place will not only help deliver much-needed homes, it will also bring new energy and life, revitalising neighbourhoods and helping to build stronger, more resilient communities," said BDP.

16 June 2021

Grenfell: four years after the disaster, are our buildings safer?

An article from The Conversation.

By Paresh Wankade, Professor of Leadership and Management, Edge Hill University

THE CONVERSATION

In the four years since the Grenfell Tower fire, which led to the unconscionable deaths of 72 people, one key question remains unanswered. Are our buildings any safer? The short answer is: not yet.

The facts and figures uncovered in the ongoing Grenfell Tower inquiry and other investigations, continue to shock. An initial key finding of the inquiry's first report in 2019 was that the external cladding that surrounded Grenfell Tower was largely responsible for the fire spreading so quickly.

Since the fire, over 400 other high rise buildings surveyed around the country have been found to have external wall materials similar to those used on Grenfell Tower. Several more recent tower block fires also show serious fire hazards in high-rise buildings remain.

The Grenfell inquiry's recommendations so far have focused, primarily, on fire-safety legislation, the readiness and operational challenges of emergency services and, crucially, on how everyone – from developers to the London Fire Brigade (LFB) – needs to have a better grasp of how high rises are built and the challenges they pose.

Understanding high rises

There's still a long way to go in terms of assessing existing buildings, and ensuring their inhabitants' safety. This will require a joined-up strategy on part of the government, fire services, builders and manufacturers to ensure fire safety in high-rise buildings.

Much has been written about how the Grenfell tragedy showed that lessons from the Lakanal House, which killed six people in a south London tower block eight years earlier, were not heeded. The Fire and Rescue Service in general, and its fire-risk assessments in particular, were shown to be inadequate.

To prevent such a tragedy from happening again, the state has put £1.6 billion towards dealing with unsafe cladding systems on residential buildings of 18 metres and over. Before COVID hit, the government pledged to inspect and review all high-rise buildings in England by the end of 2021. It is not clear to what extent the pandemic has hampered that process.

The government is also supporting research into evacuation strategies in blocks of flats. This follows Moore-Bick's call for an end to the the "stay put" directive which proved so disastrous for the residents of Grenfell Tower.

Fire safety regulations

New fire safety laws that have been passed are a welcome development, but they will require investments and expertise in fire services to undertake additional inspections and reviews.

The inquiry criticised the government's Fire and Rescue Service for not understanding how combustible external cladding was. It highlighted the absence of a regulatory framework to share and store information about fire-safety features. It also warned about the absence of a national evacuation strategy for high-rise buildings.

In response, the government has taken prompt actions. In February it named Peter Baker as the UK's first chief inspector of buildings, to run a new national regulator of building safety. As specified in the draft Building Safety Bill 2020, Baker is tasked, in particular, with appointing an "accountable person" for every high rise in England. Their role will be to listen and respond to residents' concerns, giving access to vital safety information to residents and leaseholders

Further, the newly enacted Fire Safety Act 2021 improves on previous legislation, by making the owners of high rises and other residential blocks responsible for managing the fire risk of certain key elements. This includes the structure and the external walls of the building, including cladding, balconies and windows, as well as the entrance doors to individual flats that open into communal areas.

Better training

The LFB still has a lot of crucial work to do. The inquiry was very critical of the fact that the otherwise experienced incident commanders and senior officers who attended the scene had received no training in the particular dangers associated with combustible cladding. It also criticised the brigade's evacuation strategies, and lack of contingency plans.

The Mayor of London's monthly progress reports do show some progress has been made. In particular, policy on how emergency responders are trained to distinguish between callers seeking advice and those needing to be rescued, and on communications between incident commanders and the control room has been revised.

However, the latest independent assessment, carried out by Her Majesty's Inspectorate of Constabulary and Fire & Rescue Services, expressed concerns that only a handful of the inquiry's recommendations were actually completed. It highlighted staff shortages causing delays.

Coordinating emergency responses

The inquiry found the different emergency responders (the LFB, the Metropolitan Police and the London Ambulance Service) failed to work together in an efficient way. And, so far, very little has changed.

Crucially, each declared a major incident independently, and without informing the others. This meant that the need for a properly coordinated response was not appreciated in time.

The report stressed the urgent need for clear lines of communication – and compatible tech – between the control rooms of individual services. It detailed how communication between the emergency services on the night of the fire, both remotely and on the incident ground itself, did not meet the standards required by existing fire safety protocols. The communication link with the police helicopter overhead failed to function, which also adversely affected LFB operations.

It noted that a single point of contact in each control room and direct communication between control room supervisors should have been established. A review is currently underway to address these recommendations.

Much to be done

In sum, for our buildings to be safer and those of us who live in them to feel more secure, there remains a lot to be done. Removing unsafe cladding and installing fire safety features in older buildings is a painfully slow process.

Quite who is responsible for paying for this work is an unresolved question too. Leaseholders and residents could yet end up footing the bill. Leaseholders of that east London tower that caught fire in May remain liable for £3.1m of the £11.6m cost to fix their building complex.

Critics have slammed the politicians for letting the developers off the hook and passing on the burden of responsibility. Many resident groups have called this out as a grave injustice.

Unless the lessons from Grenfell are learned and prompt action is taken, we may fail the Grenfell residents who lost their lives four years ago.

14 June 2021

Changing attitudes to second home ownership

The number of people who own a second home has risen 33% in ten years according to data from the English Housing Survey.

In 2018/19 there were 3.75 million second properties – up from 2.68 million a decade earlier. However attitudes to second home ownership are changing as the survey shows in 2018/19, 35% of second property owners thought of it as a long-term investment. Five years prior, this was 48%.

And the number of people who owned second homes as holiday homes has decreased as the buy-to-let market has grown.

Sarah Coles, personal finance analyst, Hargreaves Lansdown:

"The second home dream is alive and well. Despite rising prices, more than a million have been snapped up in the past decade alone. But most people aren't planning a strategic property portfolio to make their millions, many have either realised their dream of owning a holiday home, or stumbled into becoming accidental landlords.

"When asked why they had a second home, more people said they wanted it as a holiday home than said they saw it as a long-term investment. The proportion who claimed to be investing has dropped 5 percentage points in a decade – and is down 13 percentage points from a spike in 2013/14. This may have something to do with the fact that this period saw sluggish property price rises, so owners were aware it might not make their fortune. The government has also worked hard to make property investment as unrewarding as possible from a tax perspective. Since 2016 there has been extra stamp duty to pay when you buy, and since 2017 the rules on offsetting mortgage interest against tax on rental income have made this far less attractive too. It means you're taxed on the way in, as you go along, and when you sell, so it's one of the least tax-efficient

ways to invest. When you compare it to ISAs, which are completely tax free, the tax burden is enormous

"One strong trend we've seen is the rise in people who said their second property was previously their main home. Now that couples are marrying later, and more people have more complex family relationships, they're more likely to come to a relationship either with a property they have bought alone or a share in a former marital home. In some cases, you're legally required to hang onto that property as the result of a divorce settlement.

"However, if you're renting it out for an income stream, it's worth doing the calculations to ensure that even after maintenance, void periods and tax, you're making enough profit to make it worthwhile."

The survey also identified that the most common reason for owning a second property is still as a holiday home – at 39%. However, this is down from 50% a decade earlier.

The Welsh Government recently announced a crackdown on second home ownership citing communities decimated by the influx of holiday home ownership. Since 2017 councils have been able to place a premium on council tax for second homes in Wales and second home buyers already face higher stamp duty costs.

The latest proposals are designed to address the issue of affordability for local buyers, regulate the sale of second homes with a system of registration for holiday homes, and ensure second home owners make a fairer contribution to the local economy.

19 July 2021

Second homeowners are harming local communities and the planet

In addition to the climate impacts, owning a second home has damaging social consequences. By Donnachadh McCarthy

It is harder for a rich holiday homeowner than a camel to get through the eye of the zero carbon needle.

In a recent speech in parliament, the Liberal Democrat MP Tim Farron equated the impact of rocketing second home ownership in Cumbria with the 19th century Scottish land clearances, when the aristocracy swept tenant farmers off their ancestral lands and replaced them with sheep. He said that whole towns and villages across his constituency were becoming second home ghost towns.

Farron's speech brings the plethora of destructive impacts of second home ownership on communities, young people, nature and climate destruction into the public eye.

It was only when regional airline Flybe was going bankrupt and I read an interview with a "victim" in London, complaining she could no longer fly every weekend down to her holiday home in Cornwall, that I twigged that second homeowners were a significant source of UK aviation emissions.

This was reinforced when I recently did a joint interview on BBC Radio with a famous business person on the pros and cons of a frequent flyer tax, which would impose an increasing tax on those taking multiple flights each year.

Whilst I waxed lyrical about the peace and quiet the lockdown pause to Heathrow airport had brought to my back garden last summer, the businessman raged that I should instead be focusing on Chinese carbon emissions rather than on UK frequent flyers.

So, I asked him how often he flew and he admitted to flying at least 15 times a year to his holiday home in Spain.

There are an estimated 500,000 Britons with second homes abroad in Europe. Let us say on average they are a four-person family and fly six times a year to their second home.

That would equate to 24 million high carbon international flights every year!

A family of four's return flight to Turkey would emit about four tonnes of CO_2. Six trips a year would emit 24 tonnes. This is the equivalent of 30 years of the average UK household's electricity carbon emissions. Then there are the emissions from those flying or driving to second homes in the UK itself.

Research by AIG found that the super-rich in the US have up to nine foreign holiday homes spread around the world. Flights between them will often be done by private jet.

These can emit about 2 tonnes of CO_2 per hour in-flight.

Then there are the embedded carbon emissions in the buildings themselves. The emissions from building the average UK home are estimated to be about 65 tonnes.

Having a second home can thus double their embedded homeownership emissions per family, depending on its size, to 130 tonnes.

Then there is the duplication of household furnishings and other possessions, including lawnmowers, washing

machines, ovens, crockery and so on. The wood, steel, glass, concrete, sand and precious metals for these will all result in additional carbon emissions and exacerbate negative mining impacts, deforestation and the destruction of our few remaining wildlife habitats.

In addition to the climate impacts, owning a second home has damaging social consequences, not only on the community where their second property is located but also in their home community. If you spend four days per week working from your city home and the rest at your holiday home, you end up hurting both communities.

From Cornwall to Wales, from Norfolk to Cumbria, local communities are being destroyed by second homeownership. It artificially pushes house mortgages to soar above what a local working class wage can afford and forces out local young people.

Up to 10 per cent of homes in parts of rural Wales are now holiday homes and there are an estimated 13,000 second homes in Cornwall. There is a particular problem with the influx of non-Welsh speaking second homeowners into rural Welsh speaking areas, endangering the language.

Pouring salt on local community wounds, George Monbiot recently reported that instead of punitive taxation for second homes to protect local communities, the government is actually fuelling their destruction. Second homeowners get a raft of tax exemptions, including the writing off of mortgages as holiday let business expenses and often avoiding council taxes altogether.

So what needs to be done? Our climate, nature and rural communities simply cannot afford this destructiveness. A sliding scale of punitive taxes needs to be imposed on every extra flight taken over a year, or better still, a flight emissions rationing system put in place.

All tax exemptions for second home ownership, including Airbnb, need to be abolished and replaced with a community charge at least three times the local rate. And finally, as Tim Farron rightly calls for, instead of the government enacting the current proposed abolition of most of our planning protections, it needs to create a new planning category for second homes and holiday rentals.

The owners would have to apply for planning permission to have a second house in the community or to rent it out as a holiday home. The local community would then be able to protect their often centuries-old identities and cultures.

It is time to end the climate, ecological and social destruction by the elite second home owning classes.

7 August 2021

Blueprint for future of UK housing unveiled

£400m is earmarked to help build homes on brownfield sites and to redevelop empty high streets for housing.

By Richard Reed

A blueprint for the future of new housing in the UK has been unveiled by the government.

Key to the proposals is a bid to identify and redevelop unused urban brownfield sites, while avoiding lengthy planning delays.

Councils will also be told to put housing needs first when redeveloping high streets left empty by retail decline – and to encourage high-rise developments near rail, tube and tram stations.

Next month the government will launch a register of brownfield sites which will map out unused land as part of plans to encourage councils to prioritise this land over greenfield sites – backed by £400m to bring this mostly unused land back to use.

Developers will be able to demolish vacant commercial, industrial and residential buildings and replace them with well-designed homes without getting delayed in a lengthy planning process, meaning that more homes will be delivered more quickly.

Green design

Good design will be at the heart of the new system, with the government championing tree-lined streets, a 'fast track for beauty', and a commitment to lower carbon emissions in all new homes to create a green revolution in housebuilding.

The government will review how councils assess how many homes are needed in their area and incentivise those that deliver on those numbers.

All local authorities will be required to have up-to-date Local Plans in place by December 2023, or see government intervention, so enough homes are built for their communities.

The changes come ahead of plans for an ambitious planning white paper – set to radically reform the planning system by speeding up the decision-making process so homes can be built more quickly where they are most needed.

Levelling up

Housing Secretary Robert Jenrick said: "I want everyone, no matter where they live, to have access to affordable, safe, quality housing and live in communities with a real sense of

place – as part of our mission to level up, unite and unleash the potential of this country.

"We must think boldly and creatively about the planning system to make it fit for the future, and this is just the first step, so we can deliver the homes communities need."

The announcement follows a package of measures announced in yesterday's Budget to help more people onto the housing ladder by building more affordable homes and speeding up the planning process to deliver the 300,000 homes a year the country needs.

There will be help for those that want to build their own home, and for parish councils and neighbourhood forums wanting to build a small number of homes that will allow their community to grow.

There will also be an allocation of £1.1bn from the Housing Infrastructure Fund to help build nearly 70,000 new homes in high-demand areas across the country.

There will also be £12bn of investment to build more affordable homes, with the ability to also bring in around £38bn of further private and public investment.

13 March 2020

Why Britain's newbuilds are so ugly

£400m is earmarked to help build homes on brownfield sites and to redevelop empty high streets for housing.

By Richard Reed

A new housing estate is being built outside your town. What do you hope it looks like? Britain's housing stock includes everything from stone cottages to the pair of new skyscrapers in Nine Elms, south London, connected to one another by a swimming pool "bridge" suspended 115ft in the air. Elsewhere we have neo-classical Georgian townhouses, arts and crafts-influenced semis, Victorian terraces, brutalist tower blocks, the boxy brick houses of modern suburban developments and much else. So which would you choose to drive past every day? Which would you choose to live in?

The Government has an inkling. "Poll after poll suggests we prefer the homes built before planning really began with the 1947 Planning Act, not those that came after," Housing Secretary Robert Jenrick said in a July speech to the Policy Exchange think tank. Weeks later, Nicholas Boys Smith, a senior adviser to Jenrick, told a conference that nobody should condemn the Not In My Back Yard brigade for their "emotional" response to homes being built on their doorsteps, saying: "If we can understand better what concerns Nimbys and to some degree work with them, we can create better, more lovable and more sustainable and greener places."

In July Jenrick and Boys Smith unveiled the new National Model Design Code and a revised National Planning Policy Framework while also launching the Office for Place within the Ministry of Housing to help local authorities across England create design codes that will give residents a say in the design of new developments in their areas. These three elements are intended to enable the construction of "beautiful, high-quality homes" built in keeping with local conventions, whether that be the red brick of northern towns or the masonry of the south.

The Government has committed to delivering 300,000 homes a year across England by the mid 2020s and what Jenrick and co seem to be trying to do with this latest move is alleviate the housing crisis without wreaking aesthetic destruction on our towns, cities and countryside. But it raises many questions: why did housing get so ugly? How do we define beauty? Will the new rules lead to naff pastiche, glorious neo-traditionalism, or just a continuation of the status quo? Was Prince Charles right when, back in 1984, he castigated modern architecture and called for a return to traditional building styles?

"The Government correctly believes that the ugliness of new development is one major reason why people oppose it," says Dr Samuel Hughes, a senior fellow at Policy Exchange and an academic philosopher working as a research fellow at the University of Oxford. He was research assistant to the Building Better, Building Beautiful commission chaired by Boys Smith and the late philosopher Sir Roger Scruton – whose report, published in January 2020, provided many of the ideas in the strategy recently unveiled by Jenrick. Hughes, 29, is giving me an architectural tour of Muswell Hill in north London. We start at St James's church. Opposite is Muswell Hill Broadway, whose sweep of four-storey Edwardian buildings is rudely interrupted by an ugly, cuboid block of flats, dating perhaps from the 1960s, that looms above a Sainsbury's. This "monster", as Hughes jocularly puts it, sits where a handsome music hall once stood.

"That would not happen now," says Hughes, pointing out that today's planning rules are more protective of aged finery. But the most important change since the construction of the Edwardian buildings, he says, is that the road is now filled with cars. "In 1905, you had a little bit of wheeled transport coming through, going at 5mph, no faster than the pedestrians. They didn't have road crossings because they didn't need them. So this would all have been a space into which we naturally would have walked."

Today the road is clogged by traffic whose noise is loud enough to impair our conversation. "It's not exactly a nice place to be and that's because of the constant traffic."

On a quieter road, with terraces of Victorian houses on each side, Hughes explains the difficulties the car poses to neighbourhood design. A couple who buy a house in a new development will often have a car each. That's two parking spaces. They might want space for a guest (three spaces) and they might end up with teenagers with cars of their own (four or more). "It starts to force the houses apart and to create these more Tarmac-y spaces that we're familiar with." Thus bustling streets become roads, houses become more atomised, house prices go up as a result of the extra land requirements, and a walk to the shops becomes a drive.

We will be dependent on cars for the foreseeable future but there are measures we might take to reduce their influence. A small start that Hughes suggests is studding the road edges with trees: "You'd end up with a visually narrower carriageway and really strengthen the sense that this is a space for pedestrians."

On an Edwardian residential street, Hughes points out gables featuring pastoral mouldings and detailing done in a mock-18th-century style, "downstream from the Queen Anne style, aiming at a slightly idealised version of England's past". At the time of these houses' construction, he says, the snobs of the day would have looked down on them. But although the builders were playing to putatively unsophisticated tastes, they "created something that's beautiful and has stood the test of time".

Today's housebuilders are no more villainous or stupid or greedy than those of the past, Hughes insists; the problem is simply "a defective development control system that means what they're incentivised to do is build something people don't particularly welcome".

Hughes gives the impression of being a young fogey without evincing the views of one.

Among his favourite sights on our 90-minute tour is a recently completed development in a contemporary style featuring two uneven rows of grey-brick terraced houses separated by a paved and almost car-less street, which he says create "a pleasing environment, almost like a medieval town".

Where are the cars? "There are no undercrofts in Heaven," Hughes says of what turns out to be underground car parking, "but this development, on the whole, makes me optimistic."

Later, a block of flats, with hedges shielding it from the road, catches his eye. "It's a good, ordinary, interwar mansion block. There is very little here that should not be easily reproducible: an attractive facing brick; a straightforward façade pattern; standard sash windows. [It has] no rare materials, no exquisite craftsmanship and no inspired design – and that's the point: it's a good vernacular; a good normal."

Hughes isn't rooting for the revival of any particular style. "It's about empowering local people," he says, "but I suspect we won't see a wave of brutalism sweeping the country."

I imagine he is right. The extent of the difference is sometimes exaggerated, but the public does tend to have more traditional taste than the architects behind some of the more outré manifestations of modernist and postmodernist building designs. Hughes cites the much-loved Sydney Opera House as a counterexample, but refers to research that shows the longer students study architecture, the more at odds they become with public rankings of beautiful buildings.

This gulf between professional and public is probably true of most art forms, I venture. Hughes agrees. "Atonal classical music is greatly respected by highly-trained people, but almost nobody listens to it. There is a near-total lack of interest from ordinary people."

The difference is that you can generally make it down the street without being subjected to music you dislike.

On the one hand, pleasing architecture can reinforce local character and win round any Nimbys: an example of a third-party benefit, or "positive externalities", to use the lingo.

On the other, "negative externalities" can do exactly the opposite. So will increased public involvement as a result of the new regulations be enough to dispel Nimbyism?

Hughes doesn't think so, but he hopes it will contribute and observes that beauty comes with sustainability. "If people don't tear it down, they're spared the enormous carbon cost of constructing a new building."

Over the course of our walk, Hughes has given me an education in edifice, finding delight in almost every building he sees. Some element of the art of beautifying our neighbourhoods, I realise, is observing what beauty is already there. In that spirit, it is worth examining why those boxy brick detached houses so commonly found in new developments look the way they do. They seem exactly the kind of generic construction that the new rules are designed to counter, but they sell by the hundreds of thousands every year.

According to Andrew Whitaker, planning director of the Home Builders Federation, the trade body for private-sector developers in England and Wales, these house shapes are a product of the regulations that govern the inside of the house, "like mobility standards, like internal space standards".

As for the generic look of the exterior, while it is easier and cheaper to create than a Georgian or Victorian style, it also seems to be what people want. "If you ask kids to draw a house, they'll draw the Play School house, with a door in the middle, windows each side, and a pitched roof," says Whitaker. "Lots and lots of people have that concept; that this is what a house looks like. They don't think of Marmalade Lane."

Marmalade Lane, a modern development in Cambridge complete with a car-free lane and facilities shared between residents, has drawn praise for its designers Mole Architects.

Among its admirers is Roland Karthaus, director of Matter Architecture and a member of the Royal Institute of British Architects' expert advisory group for planning, who approves of its shared spaces, intergenerational mix and "reasonably contemporary interpretation of traditional domestic architecture".

Karthaus stresses that the design of new developments should not just be about the houses themselves. "What we need are well-designed places," he says. Putting cars first "is a first-order mistake". What is needed, he argues, are coherent neighbourhoods. "It's all of the houses together; the facilities that are there; the scale and quantity of the services that are provided; the transport – all of those things together, at the scale that you experience it. What does it actually feel like to walk out your front door and be able to walk to the corner shop and bump into somebody on the way and sit in a park?"

Beauty, Karthaus suggests, might have more to do with how something works than its skin-deep aesthetics. He praises the Georgians, not for any particular visual convention of their era – they also built bad buildings that have not been preserved – but because they invested long-term interest in places and ensured that local architecture was harmonious.

"They invented the leaseholder system and a particular form of design code," Karthaus says. "That's a much more important thing to understand than simple aesthetics."

Long-term landowner interest doesn't come much longer-term than the Duchy of Cornwall. Poundbury (see below), a Dorchester-adjacent town extension whose architecture ranges from Georgian to neo-classical and whose layout is designed for pedestrians' ease, is built on Duchy land and owes its existence at least in part to Prince Charles. It has been maligned since its 1993 launch as being reactionary, but one of its leading architects, Ben Pentreath, tells me its success is a vindication of the prince's views, which "have been proved visionary".

Referring to his Tornagrain project near Inverness, in which elegant whitewashed homes line steep streets with views of surrounding hills, Pentreath advocates design led by landscape. He would also like to see huge investment in the role of local authority planners, funded by increasing planning costs.

Pentreath suggests introducing a simple national pattern book with which to influence the design teams of the five major housebuilders whose small teams of designers – which he says amount to a total of 20 or 30 people – decide the look of nearly all new homes in Britain. "Whenever I've met some of them, I've found them to be nice, well-meaning people, who unfortunately don't quite always know how to really proportion a window or design a well-made simple door surround."

He applauds the sense of purpose spurred by the new rules, but notes: "I do worry they will join a huge pile of beautifully written documents and legislation that have been produced

since at least the 1920s by very well-meaning architects and politicians who want to make changes.

"Somehow I fear the world as it is will carry on doing what it does."

Housing by numbers

♦ 144,000: The number of private sector homes built in England in 2019, according to the ONS

♦ 244,000: The 2020 new homes total in England

♦ 300,000: Government target for annual housebuilding in England by mid-2020

♦ 340,000: The National Housing Federation's estimate of England's yearly need

What a neighbourhood needs for its people to thrive

Sir Roger Scruton, who died last year, was one of the leading thinkers behind the new strategy. He wrote: "We have a need for friends, family and physical contact; we have a need to pass people peacefully in the street, to greet each other and to sense the safety of a cared-for environment that is also ours. The sense of beauty is rooted in these feelings, and it is the principal reason why people fight to preserve it."

In keeping with the principle that villages, towns and cities should be pedestrian-friendly, urban planners approve of places that pass the "pint of milk test" – can a resident walk to a shop to buy a pint of milk in 10 minutes or less?

Designers, architects and scientists agree that we need lots of natural light, views of and access to nature, clean air and minimal levels of noise pollution. We also benefit from having friendly interactions, however brief, with people we don't know well but see regularly.

How to have your say on that local development

What am I allowed to do?

The Government's guidance on the new National Model Design Code says that developers and local planning authorities must give local communities every opportunity to participate in the creation of new local codes. So if you have a neighbourhood planning group, join it.

How do I comment on a planning application?

After a council receives a planning application there is a consultation period, usually 21 days or more, in which local people can express their views. Your council should have an online list of applications. Address your response to the planning department and quote the planning application number.

What counts as a valid objection?

Councils will take into account loss of light and overshadowing; overlooking and loss of privacy; loss of trees; an effect on listed buildings and conservation areas; nature conservation; design, appearance and materials; and traffic generation, highway safety, and noise and disturbance

resulting from the use of the competed building. Councils will not take into account the loss of a view, or a reduction in local house prices.

How can I encourage good construction?

Beyond that, you can join or set up a local branch of the Yimby Alliance (Yimby, of course, standing for "Yes, in my backyard"). Visit yimbyalliance.org.

Around every corner in Poundbury you will find something different – from the Edwardian to the Victorian to the really modern industrial-looking buildings just off Peverell Avenue. I grew up 10 miles away in Weymouth and always liked what was happening in Poundbury.

Eight years ago, I started a business in Poundbury – Boo's Toy Shop – and it made sense for me and my partner to move here. We now live in a lovely pastel-yellow home on a square in the North East Quadrant, which is still being developed. Our neighbours have buildings in pink and green, so this area is a really pretty injection of colour.

In some towns, and even in the older parts of Poundbury, you don't have much green space, but in addition to our own beautiful garden we have access to the square beside our house, which is a gated area with park benches and greenery. Soon there'll be even more green space, because the builders are developing the Great Field, which will have lots of tall trees and wildflowers as well as a play park and a cafe.

It's the perfect place for us, and a big part of that is the lovely community. We are close to our neighbours and everyone is kind and courteous.

When you build a new town, you can set the scene of how you would like it to develop over time, and I think the people who did that here in Poundbury did a fantastic job. There's a similar site being built in Cornwall called Nansledan and their residents' association came to visit ours to ask questions about how to develop a community.

The other thing that makes a massive difference here is that Poundbury is designed to be easy to walk around in. There are lots of footpaths and the distinctive architecture makes it simple to find your way. Where I live, I'm a three-minute walk from the Great Field and a five-minute walk from the butcher's and Waitrose. I'm a three-minute walk from my shop, too – but I can't deny I get in my car when it's raining!

In the early days, there was a lot of negativity about Poundbury but you're never going to please everybody with different architecture and different ways of living. I think that what Prince Charles has created, with the help of the architects and the Duchy of Cornwall, is amazing. I've been fortunate enough to meet him on two occasions. He's very kind, very caring, and very interested in what is happening in the area.

One of the most serious things about old age, especially if you become less mobile, is isolation and loneliness. That's not what my husband Wayne and I wanted for ourselves.

He's from Canada, where it's more common to see co-housing developments [private homes clustered around community space that may include shared kitchen, dining, laundry or recreational facilities], and friends of ours who live in them love the sense of purpose and activity. So we went for a house in Marmalade Lane in 2019.

In London we hardly knew our neighbours, but Marmalade Lane is designed so that you interact with people you live with. Because there are no cars on the lane you can stand around and chat to people. Garden walls are low so you can sit outside with a coffee and someone will say hello, and the backs of one row of houses face the fronts of the other row rather than each facing away from the other, as is usually the case. There's a shared garden, laundry, allotment, workshop and an intentionally sharing community working together to run it in ways that are good for us all and for the planet.

Most of us like the clean, modern look of the place, although we're trying to make it greener and to get more creeping plants growing on some of this brick. As our summers get warmer, more trees and more greenery will help keep the lane cool. With features like air source heat pumps and good insulation, the houses are designed to help us live more sustainably. Lots of residents have their own cars in the car park, but there's also a car club with two small cars, one of them electric.

Living somewhere like this is a fantastic way to really be part of the community. It's great for older people like us, it's great for single people because it's sociable and it's also great for all the young families here who are bringing up their children in a much more relaxed and easy environment than you would get in a normal urban or suburban street.

5 September 2021

Eco-homes become hot property in UK's zero-carbon 'paradigm shift'

Smart, low-carbon homes were once the preserve of one-off grand designs – now there are up to 30,000 projects in the pipeline.

By Oliver Wainwright

Instead of parking spaces, it's flowerbeds and vegetable planters that line the car-free street of Solar Avenue in Leeds, where rows of 60 low-energy homes form a little oasis along a bend in the River Aire, a short walk from the city centre.

Built in a factory across the road, these terrace houses are made from super-airtight timber panels stuffed full of wood-fibre insulation, with triple-glazed windows and solar panels on the roof, each erected in less than a week. Using up to 10 times less energy than a conventional house, their heating demand is so low that they create excess electricity that is fed into a community grid and used to charge shared electric cars. There will soon be 1,000 such homes here, along with a combined primary school and care home, as well as a timber office building with yoga decks and a tennis court on the roof, together forming the pioneering Climate Innovation District.

A few years ago these houses would have been experimental one-offs. But a green-design campaign group has calculated there are as many as 30,000 low-carbon homes in the pipeline, an impressive turnaround in which the industry is leading the way, ahead of government regulation.

"The way we build housing in the UK hasn't changed much since the Victorian era," says Chris Thompson, the founder of Citu, the developer behind the Leeds project, which plans to build 500 low-energy homes a year. "It's all driven by perceived risk. Anyone looking to build something has to answer to a funder, who'll use valuers to ensure that what you're proposing has a market."

Shifting the mindset of such a risk-averse industry can seem like an insurmountable challenge, not helped by the government dragging its heels on policy changes. But now, after scrapping Labour's zero-carbon homes target in 2015, the Conservative government has finally developed a future homes standard, which will mandate all new homes to be "zero-carbon-ready" – although not until 2025 at the earliest.

So it has been the landlords with a long-term interest in the wellbeing of their tenants, and the longevity of their building stock, who are forging ahead with low-energy housing.

Exeter city council, for example, has been quietly building zero-carbon homes for the last decade, with more than 200 council houses built so far to the exacting Passivhaus low-energy standard, and 1,000 more in the pipeline.

"We were originally driven by trying to address fuel poverty," says Emma Osmundsen, director of the council's housing company, Exeter City Living. "Not many people were talking about climate change in 2009, when we built our first three Passivhaus homes, so we became a kind of accidental pioneer." The council is now on the seventh generation of its low-energy house design, which it has honed over the years to make it as "idiot-proof" as possible, says Osmundsen. Rather than timber frame, they use clay blocks that slot together like Lego bricks and contain a honeycomb of air pockets, negating the need for additional insulation. The homes are so thermally efficient that 60% of the tenants haven't had to switch on their heating at all – some for more than 12 years.

Like many in the industry, she thinks the biggest barrier to wider adoption of low-energy standards is the lack of care and attention to detail on British building sites. "Passivhaus

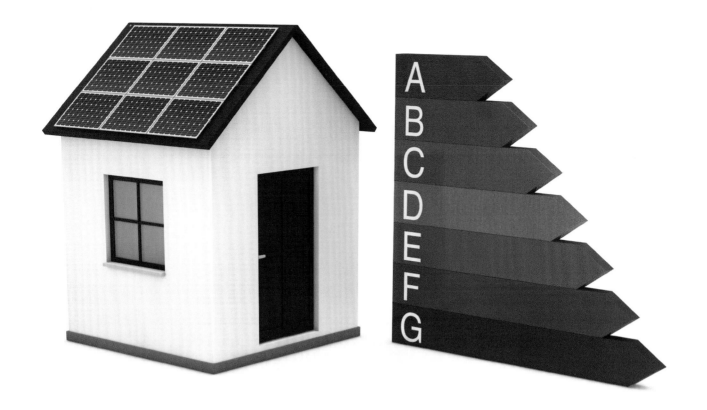

is really not complicated, and it doesn't have to cost more than conventional construction," she says. "It's a bit like baking a cake: most of the ingredients are the same as a regular house, but you just have to follow the recipe in the right order. Perhaps it's because the building industry is so male-dominated, but there is a general reluctance to follow the recipe."

Many other councils are following Exeter's lead. Norwich completed the country's largest Passivhaus social housing scheme in 2019, winning the prestigious RIBA Stirling Prize in the process, while York is planning an even more ambitious scheme by the same architects, Mikhail Riches. Cardiff University built an "energy positive" solar house in 2015, using low-cost, off-the-peg materials, with features that have since been replicated in more than 1,400 affordable and low-carbon houses across Wales. Oxford has started work on its first zero-carbon council homes, while Enfield council's huge £6bn Meridian Water development is also targeting net zero.

"It used to feel like we were ploughing a lone furrow," says Jon Bootland, the chief executive of the Passivhaus Trust, which was established over a decade ago to promote the low-energy standard, but for years was seen as the preserve of one-off eco-homes in the countryside. "Now our approach is really in the mainstream, as one of the few proven routes to net zero." The non-profit organisation, which trains designers and contractors and certifies buildings, has recorded a 60% increase in membership over the last year alone.

The environmental engineer Clara Bagenal George, the founder of the London Energy Transformation Initiative (Leti), has calculated that there are now about 30,000 homes at the masterplan stage that meet the Passivhaus target for a space heating demand of just 15 kWh/sq metre/year (compared with the current average of 54 kWh/sq metre/year), equating to a massive reduction in carbon. "It's an amazing story," she says. "The industry defined 'good', over and above the regulations, and within a year there are now tens of thousands of homes in the works that meet this standard. It shows we can do it."

And even the volume housebuilders are starting to get on board. "It's almost paradigm shift territory," says Simon Usher, divisional director of Persimmon Homes, one of the largest developers in the country, which infamously paid its former chief executive a £75m bonus in 2018, while its homes were found to be riddled with construction defects.

In 2019 the company admitted it had lobbied the government to axe its zero-carbon policy, but, in an effort to clean up its image, with a new chief executive at the helm, it is now working on a prototype zero-carbon house of its own near its headquarters in York.

"It's an unashamedly normal house," says Usher. "We wanted to see how far we could get with our standard masonry construction, building with our usual concrete bricks and tiles, but adding more insulation, beefing up the windows a bit, and adding an air-source heat pump in the garden. In the end, we got to zero carbon, for about 15% additional cost."

"People are willing to pay more for an electric car to do the right thing," says Usher. "Will they be willing to do the same for a zero-carbon home? The market will decide."

6 March 2021

Eco-friendly homes: a look at millennials and the housing market

As millennials hit the housing market, the construction of 'wellness-minded' buildings and eco-friendly homes are on the rise.

With solar panels in the roofs and built with environmentally friendly materials, green buildings have become popular not just amongst millennials, but with celebrities too.

Orlando Bloom, Prince Charles and Damien Hurst all have sustainable homes and the number continues to rise.

Developed to have a limited effect on the environment, eco-friendly homes are built to be as self-sufficient as possible. Using many natural resources such as light, wind and earth, sustainable homes aim to lower their carbon footprint and significantly reduce the amount of heat and power a homeowner consumes.

Economically insulated by incorporating earthbags, logs, stones, recyclables, bamboo and straw, eco-friendly homes cause significantly less damage to the surrounding environment. Other benefits include:

♦ Lower maintenance requirements

♦ Consistent temperature

♦ Higher quality air (and better health)

♦ Reduced waste

♦ Reduced expenses

Why are they growing in popularity?

Sustainability is a word that has been used more frequently over the years with reducing carbon emissions and saving the environment on the top of everyone's agenda. This has caused several homeowners to relocate from traditional bricks-and-mortar houses into different types of accommodation.

Jo and Paul Morton, who live the ultimate 'low impact' lifestyle in a caravan, explain:

"Everything we do is based on reducing our carbon footprint as far as possible. Whether bathing in harvested rain water or growing cabbages to preserve as sauerkraut for winter, we plan carefully so we minimise our use of fossil fuels."

However, the changes in the way we live could mostly be down to 'green' millennials, i.e. those who were born at the beginning of the rise in interest in green attitudes and behaviour.

According to a survey conducted by The Guardian, more than two thirds of millennials 'buy as many eco-friendly products as they can' and in a recent survey 66% of global respondents say that they're willing to pay more for products and services which come from companies that are committed to a positive social and environmental impact.

Growing up in an eco-conscious society, millennials are clearly more aware of their effect on the environment and are likely to be behind the rise in eco-friendly homes.

What is the cost benefit?

Eco-friendly homes can help you save time and money as the materials used are easily accessible. Many builders are able to buy the materials locally, which not only saves time, but also reduces the carbon footprint by minimising the distance they need to be shipped.

Furthermore, using recycled materials means a lower upfront cost and construction is often quicker – materials are more likely to be available and nearby.

It is not only cheaper to build a sustainable home, but the cost of day-to-day living is also reduced. Relying on renewable energy lowers operating costs and can end up reducing the monthly bills by up to 20-30%. Saving this much a month will make a big difference to the home owner financially and there are many more cost benefits that can be explored.

Eco-friendly homes require less maintenance as they are constructed to last a long time.

Less money is spent making repairs or applying touch ups because green materials are durable and look newer for longer. The buildings' extended lifespan will also lead to a higher property value so if the homeowner decides to sell they would increase their initial investment.

In the future it is thought that both home owners and businesses will be looking into green buildings. A new breed of eco-farmhouses has already been introduced in Wales and it is likely that more operations will follow suit. Additionally, with more resources being introduced every day, eco-friendly homes will become even more accessible at a lower cost; meaning they are likely to continue to rise in popularity.

20 July 2019

George Clarke: My bold vision for the future of UK housing

The UK needs bold, ambitious action if it is to tackle its housing crisis head-on. The Big Issue asked architect, TV presenter and social homes advocate George Clarke what he would do if he was in charge of housing policy.

By Adrian Lobb

George Clarke is an architect, a very busy television presenter (currently filming FIVE series) and a committed Big Issue ambassador. He's also a proud proponent of social housing, a vocal critic of the government's housing policies, and a genuine expert when it comes to how to build for the future.

Given the housing crisis and the worrying likelihood of an imminent rise in homelessness, shouldn't we be listening to experts? We say yes. When the country is crying out for affordable, high-quality, future-proofed, ecologically sound housing – let's hear expert voices on the state of the nation's housing, on planning rules, on how we house people now and into the future. And Clarke is the expert when it comes to these things. So we asked him what he would do if he was in charge of housing policy. And over the course of 90 minutes, he offered up his expertise, passion and vision.

George Clarke: If I was in charge of housing policy...

A new plan for planning

As an urgent priority, I would change the planning system. I would make it quicker and more streamlined but still accountable in terms of design standards. The planning system and our slightly antiquated way of categorising how

people live and work is not right for 21st-century living. It hasn't caught up with the realities of how people live.

We live in a very, very different age to the time before online technology. Back then, we were at home when we were at home, and when we went to work we sat behind the desk or stood in the factory. Then, when we wanted to do leisure stuff, we went out to do that.

Now someone could be sitting in a cafe with a laptop writing a book. Or creating a piece of artwork in the foyer of a commercial building. And look at all the people working from home now – many of whom will keep working from home even after the pandemic.

The way we live and work and create things and physically use buildings has completely changed. So the Use Class system that says "that's a retail building, that's commercial, that's residential, that's light industrial" has become redundant. Obviously, you don't want someone building a light industrial building next to your bedroom but people can work and produce and make from anywhere and the system hasn't been updated.

Fix the Permitted Development Rights system

The main idea behind my new show Remarkable Renovations is converting buildings that have fallen out of use to be lived in. We've got everything from a picturesque barn in a field in Harrogate through to a high street bank and disused retail spaces.

New Permitted Development Rights rules mean certain classifications of buildings can be converted to residential use without planning. And that's good – if it's being done by good people.

If people want to produce good architecture, then those relaxed planning laws give them flexibility to get on and do it. The guys I've been meeting aren't big developers. They're people who want to create genuine family homes for themselves.

But Permitted Development Rights can get us into a very messy world, with no minimum space standards on commercial buildings being turned into residential flats. We've seen the ones I call the double-glazing-salesman-developers who say, let's get as many flats in the building as possible, we don't give a shit how small they are, how well they're designed or how maintenance-free they're going to be to live in.

Schemes have gone ahead where bedrooms don't have a window. Even prison cells have windows. So I have been lobbying the government and pushing on social media to say, Permitted Development Rights is a good thing in principle – but you have to set minimum standards. There has to be design guidance. You can't just convert a building and do what the hell you want – that can lead to slum building. In my series, we show that when it works well, it's really good.

Change the tax system to stop the dominance of Thatcher's mega-developers

If you work on an existing building, you pay 20 per cent VAT on all your building materials. For a new build, it's zero VAT. This was brought in by Margaret Thatcher, because she wanted to stimulate the economy for developers. She created all the big PLCs of today, really. Persimmon, Bellway and Barratt, the seeds for those companies were sown by Margaret Thatcher because she pushed them to "build, build, build" – on green belts, on school fields, everywhere.

The government should charge zero VAT whether it's new builds or retrofit. Why should new-build developers have a tax incentive when someone who does retrofit does not?

Bricks and mortar are our history. So many buildings in this country have got a story to tell.

In Remarkable Renovations I analyse the history. Even if it was a barn conversion, why was that barn built? What was it used for? Who was the farmer that built it? How has it changed its purpose over the years? Why did it stop being used as a barn? You get a different story each time. They're all unique. And all that history is eradicated when buildings are demolished. If we can encourage people to preserve these great buildings, with their fascinating histories, while expanding the housing stock in this country it's win-win.

Go green to counter fuel poverty

You've got companies developing all this fantastic green technology – but it's not being rolled out at scale. At the minute there is massive pushback from the big house builders against improving ecological standards in new-build homes. They don't want to do it.

Taylor Wimpey said they were not going to install clean renewable heating technology in new houses.

The government have a Renewable Heat Incentive, where residents get money back for using renewable energy, but they need to bring in a law to say developers must use green energy and recommend products. That would greatly improve the building regulations.

It makes sense for us to build in a green way. It provides additional levels of comfort in the home to the residents, reduces their energy bills and prevents fuel poverty. There are millions of people in fuel poverty, literally deciding whether to heat their house or feed their kids. People having to choose whether to eat or heat? We shouldn't be in this position in this country.

A high street revolution

I'm someone who doesn't believe really in the capitalist, globalised world. I'm pro-business and pro-profit – if you want to make a profit that's absolutely fine. But it needs to be done in a very ethical way where your staff are looked after and we've got a moral duty to be as genuinely green and sustainable as possible. Because it's frightening how much we're ripping the planet apart to just make more, more, more.

I've got a utopian dream. I don't think it's ever going to happen. But if you walk down any high street, you've just got all the same global brands – Gap, H&M, even Boots (don't get me wrong, I'm a big fan of Boots). I've got this utopian dream that they're all going to disappear to go online and all these cool, young, independent traders are going to start online businesses with a mini shop front and will be making green products and beautiful things. They won't be selling T-shirts made by kids in Vietnam, the T-shirts they sell will have been made in Stoke-on-Trent, not transported 10,000 miles with a massive carbon footprint.

Some of those massive brands would not be a big loss for us – and we could still buy from them online – but getting independent traders back on the high street would be amazing.

Fix the affordability crisis

If food had gone up by as much as housing over the last 30 or 40 years, it would cost £52 for a chicken and there would be riots in the streets. For some reason, we think it's acceptable to burden people with more and more debt when they buy a house. So it's not just a housing crisis, it's a massive affordability crisis. Young people are struggling to get jobs at the minute post-Covid, young kids' education has been affected and I am so worried about the evictions that are coming. We know for a fact that the levels of homelessness are going to go up.

I'm scared stiff about the affordability crisis. It worries the life out of me that we could have millions of young people permanently in private rented accommodation, where they don't feel stable, and feel like they can be kicked out or moved on at any point.

I was brought up on a council estate. We had absolutely nothing. But as long as my mum paid the rent every month

social housing

mixed tenure

green technology

local & sustainable manufacture

BUY LOCAL

SUPPORT YOUR COMMUNITY

to the Housing Association, we were all right. And they kept it affordable. So we felt stable and secure. It frightens the life out of me the pressures young people are going to be under.

Build more social housing

The solution is to build more social housing. But the government haven't got a clue. They are overprivileged and they're naive. They've got no idea what it's like to have nothing. We don't have enough state-owned housing to ensure the most vulnerable people in society have safe and secure housing.

If the state owned a million more houses, we could put everybody who needed them in safe and secure housing and say: we're not going to charge you rent but you need to start getting yourself back on your feet. You've got an address, now, once you've got a job we're going to start charging you minimal rent. We want to give you a hand up, we realise you're vulnerable or in a tough place, but we're going to help.

The housing is not there because we stopped building it. Right to Buy messed everything up. We had six-and-a-half million council houses across Britain, now we're at just over two million. So four million have been taken out of the system and not replaced.

You can't have 100 per cent home-ownership – which is all the government seem to care about. There are massive differences in wages and affordability. We need to have built more state housing. Now we've got nowhere for people who need help – they are all in B&Bs, temporary accommodation and honestly it breaks my heart every day.

Expand the focus from home ownership

Unfortunately our good friend [Housing Secretary] Robert Jenrick is only interested in home ownership. He doesn't care about anything else. He's got a linear way of thinking, he's dependent on the powerful big developers to build as many houses as possible (the same developers who fund the Conservative Party).

It's not about what we build, how we build or where we build. There is no council housing or state-owned housing strategy. They're not building for genuinely affordable rent.

They're not building for mixed tenure. We don't have a retrofit strategy properly funded by the Treasury, which would change everything. And Jenrick hasn't even got a self-build strategy at all.

We could have a whole generation of talented self-builders using or learning skills and trades because they want to build their own house.

So the government are very narrow-minded. They're not moving fast enough. And because of this, genuinely affordable homes that are exciting for young people to live in are not being built. It's your standard four-bedroom houses built by the big developers going up all over the countryside. They look awful. Nimbyism is rife because nobody wants to see them built in their backyards and I don't blame them.

People don't mind good-quality housing being built for their kids and grandkids. But not building rubbish for massive profits, quite often on greenbelt.

20 July 2021

The future of UK housing and the construction industry

It's been a turbulent period for the construction industry over the past year. With the ongoing pandemic and the continuing uncertainty surrounding post-Brexit trade deals, it has been somewhat difficult for companies to plan their projects.

In this article, The Access Group talks about the future of UK housing and the construction industry, and explores how housebuilders can prepare as we look ahead.

1. 300,000 homes per year

The target of building over 300,000 houses a year was set back in 2017 by the then chancellor Philip Hammond. This was further emphasised in the 2019 Conservative manifesto to "increase the number of homes being built" and stressed the need to rebalance the housing market towards more homeownership. Despite the Covid-19 pandemic, 2020 saw the delivery of houses reach numbers not seen in over three decades.

So, what does this mean for the construction industry? After all, the government's post-Covid recovery aim is to "build, build, build".

It should go without saying that this will present a number of opportunities for housebuilders, with more contracts being awarded for large housing projects. However, this has been coupled with a considerable skills shortage – workers are retiring sooner than they are being recruited. Does the industry have the talent to cope with the increasing demand?

For now, projects are having to make do with the skill sets that are currently available.

This means that managers are having to really think about how to allocate their human resources. Project management software is increasingly being adopted as it has the most accurate data available – making decision-making easier and ensuring things run more smoothly.

2. Booming housing market

Traditionally Stamp Duty is normally paid on houses over £125,000. However, over the last year, the government has increased this threshold to properties over £500,000. This may be a contributing factor to an 'incredible demand' for houses and, in turn, an increase in the cost of building work on UK homes.

The extra projects being undertaken for new builds and renovations has meant demand for essential materials such as concrete and timber has dramatically increased. Reports have suggested that record surges have been found in the price of timber, bricks and steel.

This has been exacerbated by the combined impact of Brexit and the ongoing pandemic.

While the uptake of additional projects is exciting for housebuilders, the competition for materials will increase the time it takes for them to be completed. This means that firms should be more focused on how they manage their supply chains. By utilising the right software, such as EasyBuild, managers can have the most up to date information at hand – very helpful in being able to minimise the risk of material shortages.

3. The Future Homes Standard

At the beginning of 2021, the government published the outcome of its 'Future Homes Standard' consultation. This looked to make changes to regulations in improving the energy efficiency of new homes.

The new Future Homes Standard has stated that all new homes built from 2025 will produce 75-80% less carbon emissions than homes delivered under current regulations. So how will this be implemented?

- Homes built from 2022 will produce 31% less carbon emissions.

- In 2023, the government will consult about the technical aspects of the Future Homes Standard.

- The Regulations will be updated again before coming into effect in 2025.

It goes without saying that this demonstrates a huge change for the future of UK housing and construction. Eco energy experts are drawing up plans to ensure new homes are being built in line with the new energy efficiency standards.

4. Modern Methods of Construction

'Modern Methods of Construction', or MMC, is a collective term that refers to new construction techniques that can be used as opposed to the traditional methods. As a result of the rising demand and new regulations, construction companies are always on the lookout for alternative ways to build homes.

Kit houses

The most common projects you'll see the characteristics of MMC on are those that build 'kit houses'. The majority of the manufacturing process will actually take place offsite.

Then the 'kit' will be moved to the site where it is erected. This comes with a whole host of advantages that address the challenges that the construction industry faces today. With the increasing skills and labour shortage being seen, kit houses don't require as much human resource. It also doesn't take as much time, meaning housing projects are more likely to be completed on time. However, with less design flexibility, it's not always possible to make changes at the last minute.

Modular building

Modular construction has been touted as the 'push to solve the housing crisis'. It's very similar to kit houses in the sense that a lot of the building is done offsite. A building's components are constructed in a factory before being transported to the site for assembly.

This has been praised as it's much easier to control, reducing wastage and cutting down on costs. As different aspects of a home can be built at the same time, it also reduces the time to complete a project. This is crucial to the government's aim of building 300,000 houses per year.

It is not only the new MMC techniques that are proving hugely valuable to the industry.

Technology and software, like EasyBuild, at the cutting edge of industry is increasingly being used by firms that are looking to improve productivity, project efficiency and cut costs.

5. Safety

Health and safety (H&S) should always be at the forefront of any project or construction manager's mind. What we have seen over the last five years has only gone on to prove its importance. More time and money is now being spent on checking whether applications, such as cladding, adheres to the H&S standards.

At the start of 2021, the UK government established a new regulator to ensure that construction materials are held to the highest standards of safety. It will have three main functions:

- Oversee the safer and standard of all buildings.

- Directly assure the safety of higher-risk buildings.

- Improve the competence of people responsible for managing and overseeing building work.

With the added time and responsibility for approving materials used, it would be prudent to think that it will only prolong the length of a project.

Summary

The future of UK housing and construction is going to be one with a lot of changes. With the government pledging to build 300,000 homes a year, the onus is on housebuilders to carry out a number of projects at a rate that they may not have seen before. This means they will have to look towards new ways of doing things.

Whether it's more modern techniques or through the uptake of exciting software to help with cost-cutting and efficiency. With the introduction of new standards and regulatory bodies by the UK government, the industry should be prepared for additional red tape that may increase project time.

1 July 2021

Key Facts

- Research for the National Housing Federation and Crisis, carried out by Heriot-Watt University says 145,000 affordable homes should be built annually for the next five years, of which 90,000 a year should be for social rent. This is the lowest-cost housing that councils and housing associations provide, with rents tied to local incomes. In recent times fewer than 7,000 new homes a year have been created in this category in England. (page 2)

- UK house prices have grown 160 per cent in real terms since 1996, rents are relatively high and home ownership has fallen over the past 15 years. (page 3)

- New YouGov data shows that half (53%) of Brits support a large increase in the amount of new housing being built in Britain, while 35% are opposed to the idea. (page 4)

- Research from Shelter shows the number of people affected by Britain's housing emergency is 22 million. (page 5)

- The price of renting, buying, or both in some cases, has increased faster than wages and income. According to Full Fact, the average real wage fell from the start of the global financial crash of 2008 until mid-2014. However, the average UK home now costs eight times someone's annual earnings. (page 8)

- In the financial year ending March 2020 – that is, the year before the pandemic – the median household income in the UK was £29,900. In the year to June 2021 – after the pandemic – the average price of the house that contained the average household increased by £31,000. That took it to a record high of £266,000. In other words, at a time when incomes are under pressure from a virus that has made the entire economy sick, the average house has earned more than the average household. (page 11)

- December 2020 saw yearly average UK house prices rise by 8.5%, the highest percentage increase since October 2014. (page 13)

- The number of mortgage approvals in 2020 was 818,500, a 3.7% increase. This is the largest number of approvals in a single year since 2007. (page 17)

- According to the Home Owners Alliance, 86% of people in Britain want to own their own home. (page 17)

- According to the Office for National Statistics (ONS), the average UK house price in January 2021 was £249,000. (page 18)

- Germans are, by some distance, the group most likely to eschew home ownership: two in five (42%) say they have no intention of buying property. (page 19)

- Since the 2017 Grenfell fire, over 400 other high rise buildings surveyed around the country have been found to have external wall materials similar to those used on Grenfell Tower. Several more recent tower block fires also show serious fire hazards in high-rise buildings remain. (page 22)

- In 2018/19 there were 3.75 million second properties – up from 2.68 million a decade earlier. (page 24)

- There are an estimated 500,000 Britons with second homes abroad in Europe. (page 25)

- Traditionally Stamp Duty is normally paid on houses over £125,000. (page 38)

- The new Future Homes Standard government consultation has stated that all new homes built from 2025 will produce 75-80% less carbon emissions than homes delivered under current regulations. (page 39)

Eco-home

An environmentally low-impact home designed and built using materials and technology that reduces its carbon footprint and lowers its energy needs.

Greenbelt land

A policy to prevent urban sprawls into rural areas – designates land which must remain largely undeveloped.

Housing association

Housing associations are non-profit organisations that own, let and manage affordable rental properties for people in need of a home.

Housing bubble

An increase in house prices driven by high demand and low supply in the housing market.

Landlord

The owner of a property or piece of land who rents it to another party known as a tenant.

LHA (Local Housing Allowance)

Local Housing Allowance is the rate used to calculate Universal Credit or Housing Benefit for tenants who rent from private landlords.

Micro home

A micro home is a small dwelling that is often energy-efficient and carefully designed to maximise space while minimizing its footprint. A micro home is typically suitable for one to two people.

Mortgage

A loan taken out to pay for a property which is paid back with interest.

NIMBY

A phrase for the acronym 'Not In My Back Yard'. A NIMBY is a characterisation of someone who objects to the siting of something they perceive to be unpleasant or hazardous near where they live.

Owner-occupier

An occupant who owns the home they live in.

Repossession

When a property is taken back by a bank because the property buyer has defaulted on their mortgage repayments.

Social housing

Accommodation which is owned by the government or local authority and then rented to tenants with the aim of providing affordable housing.

Stamp duty

Stamp Duty is a tax paid to the UK government when a property is bought.

Tenancy agreement

A tenancy agreement is a legal contract between a tenant and their landlord specifying the terms and conditions attached to the rental of the property.

Activities

Brainstorming

♦ As a class discuss what you know about housing in the UK.

- What is a mortgage?

- What is social housing?

- What is meant by the term 'housing bubble'?

- What does is mean to rent a property?

Research

♦ Research the cost of private renting in your area. How much do people pay on average to rent:

- a studio apartment

- a one-bed flat

- a two-bed terrace house

- a four-bed detached house.

Produce a graph to show your findings.

♦ Talk to your friends and families to find out how many people own their own properties. Make a note of the different age groups who are home-owners and how long they have taken a mortgage out for. Do any of them own more than one home? Write some notes on your findings and share with the rest of the class.

♦ Research how much money people need to buy their first home in your area. What percentage is needed for a deposit? How much are solicitors' and estate agents' fees on average? Show your findings as an infograph.

♦ In small groups, choose a country in Europe and look at their housing situation. Do more people rent than own their own property? Is there a housing shortage? Compare your findings with the rest of the class.

♦ Research the average purchase price of a 3-bedroom semi-detached house in these four cities:

- Glasgow

- Cardiff

- Belfast

- London

Produce a graph to show your findings.

Design

♦ In pairs design a micro home. Create a floorplan and label the eco-friendly aspects and space-saving tech you would like to incorporate. Share your design with the rest of the class.

♦ Choose one of the articles in this book and create an illustration that highlights its key message.

♦ You are property developer who is building 200 eco-friendly, affordable homes in your local area. In small groups design a poster or leaflet packed with information to attract potential buyers.

Oral

♦ Divide the class in half. Debate renting versus buying property. One group should argue for renting and the other for home-ownership.

♦ As a class discuss the housing crisis in the UK. What does the term 'housing crisis' mean? What are the main causes for such a crisis and what do you think can be done to overcome it?

♦ In small groups discuss the benefits and the pitfalls of living in:

- a major city

- a market town

- a small village.

Reading/writing

♦ An application has been made to build a development of 150 new houses in your village. Write a letter to your local MP giving the reasons you object to such a large-scale development. Draw attention to the impact it would have on your village's existing infrastructure and the environment.

♦ Imagine you are renting a house and your landlord is not maintaining the property properly as per the terms and conditions of your tenanacy agreement. Write a letter telling them you are not happy with the way things are being handled. List the problems with the property and suggest a meeting to discuss the issues.

♦ Read the article *Second homeowners are harming local communities and the planet* on page 25. Do you agree or disagree with the writer's viewpoint on this issue? Write your own article giving your opinion. Why do you feel this way?

Acknowledgements

The publisher is grateful for permission to reproduce the material in this book. While every care has been taken to trace and acknowledge copyright, the publisher tenders its apology for any accidental infringement or where copyright has proved untraceable. The publisher would be pleased to come to a suitable arrangement in any such case with the rightful owner.

The material reproduced in *ISSUES* books is provided as an educational resource only. The views, opinions and information contained within reprinted material in *ISSUES* books do not necessarily represent those of Independence Educational Publishers and its employees.

Images

Cover image courtesy of iStock. All other images courtesy of Freepik and Unsplash.

Illustrations

Simon Kneebone: pages 5, 21 & 34. Angelo Madrid: pages 8, 24 & 37.

Additional acknowledgements

With thanks to the Independence team: Shelley Baldry, Danielle Lobban and Jackie Staines.

Tracy Biram

Cambridge, September 2021